CALCIUM AND COMMON SENSE

CALCIUM
and
COMMON SENSE

Robert P. Heaney, M.D.
and
M. Janet Barger-Lux, M.S.

Doubleday
New York

Exercise illustrations courtesy Carol E. Goodman, M.D., "Osteoporosis: Protective Measures of Nutrition and Exercises" and *Geriatrics*.

Library of Congress Cataloging in Publication Data

Heaney, Robert Proulx, 1927–
Calcium and common sense
Robert P. Heaney and M. Janet Barger-Lux.—1st ed.
p.   cm.
Bibliography: p. 247
Includes index.
1. Osteoporosis—Popular works.   2. Osteoporosis—Prevention.
3. Calcium—Therapeutic use.   I. Barger-Lux, M. Janet.   II. Title.
RC931.O73H43   1988   87-19848
616.7′1—dc19   CIP
ISBN 0-385-24219-0

to
Rob, Murney, Barbara
Rachel, Marg, Chris and Beth,
and to
Jeff

CONTENTS

Illustrations

Preface

Miss H. called me at home one morning before I had left for the hospital. Her back was hurting her so badly she couldn't get out of her apartment. She was a retired school-teacher living on a meager pension in a federally subsidized housing project, and she had no one in the world to help her. I told her I would pick up a few things at the hospital and come see her as fast as I could.

I had known Miss H. for some time. She had osteoporosis. I had been doing research on what was happening in the bones of people with her problem, and she had spent several weeks in our bone research unit at Creighton's University Hospital while we explored how her body handled calcium.

I gathered up some novocaine and a syringe and needle at the hospital, and went to visit her. By the time I got there she had struggled to tidy up her apartment a little, but she couldn't get dressed. I knew her back pretty well. I found the sore spots and put some novocaine into them and she immediately felt better and could move more easily. I knew I wasn't curing anything, that the anesthetic would wear off in an hour or so. I hoped that, if I could break the cycle of pain-spasm-pain in her back, the relief might last a little longer than the effect of the local anesthetic. But both she and I knew it would come back. She had several badly crushed vertebrae. The damage was irreversible and permanent. Her back was deformed and we both knew she would have to live with her problem.

Though she didn't show it, I knew she was lonely and afraid, too. Afraid not just because of the pain, but because of her helplessness—especially when she had these disabling episodes of muscle spasm in the back. She had grit and a dry sense of humor, and I admired and liked her. I knew I couldn't fix what was wrong with her back. I knew, too, that I had got hold of the wrong end of the stick—that her problem had started many years earlier, long before I had first seen her or she herself had even suspected she had anything wrong.

Experience with Miss H., and with many other women like her who had volunteered to let our Creighton University team study how their bodies handled calcium, had convinced my colleagues and me that we had to start earlier. We had to study women *before* they developed their first fracture. Up till then we had been investigating what their bodies were doing with calcium, and how their bones were repairing themselves. But it was always *after* a fracture, and that told us nothing about what had led up to the fracture in the first place.

Progress in medicine has been so great in the last forty years that we sometimes forget that most of the miracles we take for granted concern the conquest of acute diseases with single causes, such as infections. Antibiotics and immunizations have all but wiped out diseases ranging from pneumococcal (lobar) pneumonia to polio. And smallpox, once the scourge of whole continents, has been totally eradicated. We still have problems with infectious disease, of course. AIDS is an example, and a reminder that we shouldn't become complacent. But infectious diseases are no longer the leading cause of death in the U.S., as they were in 1900.

What we have now is a different class of problem entirely. Cancer, high blood pressure, coronary heart disease, osteoporosis are good examples. Unlike acute infections, these are slowly developing, chronic disorders. While they often come on late in life, their roots go deep into the past. In most cases the causes have been at work for many years—maybe most of a person's lifetime—before the first symptom appears. By that time, of course, much of the damage may already have been done. While it is never too late to help someone, still, it is usually impossible to reverse the years of silent damage.

Such chronic disorders are unlike the acute ones we have so successfully conquered in another way. They usually are not specific diseases with a single, well-defined cause. They have many different causes—perhaps one responsible for the disorder in one person, another in another. But usually several different causes interact in the same person.

We have become accustomed to this kind of causal interaction in coronary artery disease in men: excess weight, high blood pressure, diet high in saturated fat, diabetes, smoking, heredity, inadequate exercise, high-cholesterol diet (at least in susceptible persons), and so forth. Each contributes to the damage—some more in certain men, others more in others. While attention to only one of those causes can help somewhat, it is usually not enough to solve the problem. In this way such disorders are clearly different from poliomyelitis, which can be so effectively prevented by a single action— being immunized against polio.

This book is about one of those chronic disorders—osteoporosis, the problem Miss H. had. Like the other chronic conditions, it usually comes on late in life. And its roots go way back to early adult life, and, for many women, even into late childhood and adolescence. Osteoporosis has many causes—most of them interacting in different patterns in different women. Like the other chronic disorders, a great deal of damage has already been done by the time the first signs appear, and it is then too late to produce a cure.

About 250,000 elderly women break their hips every year, and roughly one sixth of them die within three months. The cause of the bone fragility in these women is osteoporosis. Many women who survive hip fracture lose their independent living status and must be institutionalized—for many an outcome worse than death. More women still—though the numbers aren't accurately known—suffer spine fractures every year. The U.S. Public Health Service estimates that the 1987 monetary cost of osteoporosis to the United States was

$7–10 billion, most coming out of our financially marginal Medicare fund. And the monetary cost doesn't begin to tell the story. Many women with spine fractures develop disfiguring curvatures of the spine, constant backache, and enduring disability. Further, they have such humble incapacities as the inability to tie their shoes, pick up things off the floor, lift their grandchildren, and find clothes that fit right, not to mention the visible deformity.

No one today questions that osteoporosis is a major problem. Countless women are asking what can be done to prevent it. As for the other chronic disorders, there is no single right answer. But there is a great deal that you can do, and, more to the point, you can do it for yourself. Our purpose in this book is to help you, as a woman, make an investment in your own future. Now—before it is too late.

This book got its start in something that happened in June 1982. I had just arrived in San Francisco, and I had a fever. I had started developing typical flu symptoms on the plane, and by the time we landed, I knew I was sick. I had come to attend the annual meeting of the American Society for Bone and Mineral Research, but more specifically because I had promised the program chairperson that I would participate in a press conference the society had called for two days later.

Scientific societies are often stodgy, or seem so to the outsider. At least they don't often hold press conferences, and this was a first for this organization. The program committee had come to the conclusion that we knew things about osteoporosis that needed to be shared with the public. They had asked a group of us who had been working in this field to develop a set of commonsense recommendations. We were to present these at the press conference.

I was too sick to attend the scientific meetings, but managed to show up for the press conference, figuring I couldn't provide much more than moral support. By a series of coincidences, half of our panel failed to attend, and by default I ended up being spokesperson for the society. Maybe the fever helped my eloquence; I will never know. In any case, the press conference worked pretty well. The Associated Press put our guidelines out on the wire, and Cable News Network gave us a very good play. Osteoporosis changed overnight from an obscure disorder to a household word. And my phone hasn't stopped ringing since.

In the ensuing years I have spent countless hours, literally every week, talking on the phone to science writers, freelancers, reporters, food and health editors—all seeking to inform an interested public about calcium and about osteoporosis—or just wanting to take advantage of the latest fad. A huge amount has been written and said on the topic, and I imagine I have had direct input into much of it. For example, I was the "medical consultant" for the *Consumer Reports* story on calcium in October 1984, and I was one of Jane Brody's principal consultants for her piece in the New York *Times* in December 1985 and for Mariana Gosnell's story in *Newsweek* on January 27, 1986.

But while the public interest in osteoporosis was sparked that June in San Francisco, medical science had been studying it since the 1940s. My own involvement began in 1955, when I joined the staff of the National Institutes of Health (NIH) outside Washington, D.C., to try to find some way to use the newly available radioactive isotopes of calcium to learn about bone. To make a long story short, things worked out well. We developed a way to use the isotopes to produce useful information, and I have been working with calcium and osteoporosis ever since.

But although medical science has long known that calcium was a major component of our bones, it has not always been clear that the amount of calcium in our diet was important for bone health, even after growth was completed. In fact, when I joined the staff of the NIH in 1955, the prevailing dogma in medicine held that calcium had nothing whatsoever to do with osteoporosis. It just so happened that the senior scientist I had come to work with, G. Donald Whedon, was one of a very small group of heretics who thought that calcium had been sold short.

Nevertheless, even my faith wavered. When, in 1971, I wrote the section on bone diseases for the thirteenth edition of Cecil and Loeb (one of the two principal international textbooks of medicine), I stated that it seemed unlikely that calcium had much to do with the osteoporosis problem in humans. Since then I have had to eat those words.

By 1971 I had been a member of the faculty at Creighton for several years, and I had begun a project involving 200 nuns who had agreed to take part in a 25-year study of calcium metabolism in typical middle-aged women. I was doing what my experience with Miss H. and others like her had convinced me was necessary—studying women before they developed osteoporosis. (One might wonder how nuns qualify as typical. In some ways, of course, they aren't—principally because they don't have children. But in other important ways they are. For one thing, they get osteoporosis. That much was known. Since Vatican II, most wear ordinary dress, work out in the world at ordinary tasks, and some even smoke and drink.)

One of the first things we found, when we began to accumulate data, was that the nuns who had selected low calcium intakes in their own usual diets were losing more calcium every day than they were taking in. Since most of the calcium in the body is stored as bone, this net calcium loss meant that these women were tearing down bone before our eyes. By contrast, those with high calcium intakes tended to be in balance, and hence were not losing bone. So calcium intake was more important for protecting bone, even in the adult, than most of us had thought.

These observations had a powerful influence on scientific thinking in this field. In fact, it was our data from the studies of these nuns that led to the recommendations which were ultimately made by the NIH Consensus Conference on Osteoporosis in 1984: that middle-aged women who still had female hormones needed to take in 1,000 milligrams of cal-

cium per day, and that those who had gone through menopause and were not receiving estrogen treatment needed
1,500 milligrams per day—exactly the numbers that had
come out of our study.

Many of the science writers who have called me had the
impression that the NIH Consensus Conference and its calcium intake recommendations started what some have called
the "calcium craze." But that is not correct. Rather, it was the
fevered press conference in San Francisco in 1982 that started
the ball rolling. The spate of articles in the popular press and
the increase in the sale of calcium supplements clearly pre-
ceded the Consensus Conference.

But that wasn't their only misconception. Most really know
nothing about calcium nutrition or bone itself. After explaining the same basic material time after time, dealing with the
same misperceptions, it finally dawned on me that I ought to
tell the story myself—not just through science writers, many
of whom naturally had their own angles.

At that point I turned to a colleague, Janet Barger-Lux. She
and I had worked together for several years on various pa-
pers and projects relating to this topic. She was then directing
the Professional Services Division at Creighton's School of
Nursing, and she saw osteoporosis as very much a woman's
issue. She was distressed at the shameless exploitation of
women's fears both by the pharmaceutical ads pushing calcium supplements, and by the osteoporosis diagnostic centers
offering to measure your bone mass for you. I had learned a
great deal from her about the personal and social context of
osteoporosis, and as we talked over the book, I knew that she
would have to write some of it. She brings a rich background
that nicely complements my research focus.

Together in this book we have set about answering the
many questions we have received from the public and from
reporters. If you, too, have been confused by the "calcium
craze," *Calcium and Common Sense* will give you the information and guidance you need.

Robert P. Heaney, M.D.

1
Calcium, Bone, and You

This book is about calcium, about bone, and about what you can do both to build the strongest possible skeleton and to keep it strong throughout your life. A weak skeleton means osteoporosis, and osteoporosis means crippling fractures, typically of the spine and hip.

Osteoporosis has been estimated to afflict from 5 to 20 million people in the United States—most of them older women. It is the principal cause of skeletal fractures in the aged. There were 197,000 hip fractures in 1970. By 1980 this figure had risen to 267,000 a year. By the year 2000, the number of hip fractures is expected to reach 500,000. A woman living to age 85—a figure that many believe to be the natural human life expectancy—has about one chance in three of suffering a hip fracture, and about a fifty-fifty chance of suffering an osteoporotic fracture of some bone or other. Perhaps as many as one in six persons with hip fracture die as a result of the injury and its associated problems. Of even greater significance, hip fracture leads to the loss of independence—often to institutionalization—in about half those who survive. All too often a hip fracture tips a fragile, but well, elderly person over the edge into progressive senility and confusion.

Osteoporosis is a word that was all but unknown to the general public until just a few years ago. But it is not a new problem. Medical scientists first clearly distinguished it from other skeletal disorders nearly a century ago. Its increasing prominence in recent years is due partly to a rise in the percentage of our population living into old age. So osteoporosis, like the other disorders that are concentrated toward the end of life, is drawing appropriately increased attention. But even after adjusting for the size of the elderly population, osteoporotic fractures are becoming more common. At least two studies—one in Europe and one in North America —have reported a near doubling in the risk of hip fracture among the elderly in the years since World War II. No one knows for sure why (though this book will help you to understand some of the possible reasons). Finally, osteoporosis is predominantly a problem of women, and women's issues have been receiving more of the attention they deserve in recent years.

The annual cost of osteoporosis to the United States was estimated in 1987 to be $7–10 billion, and that figure is certain to rise much higher before we will be able to get the problem under control. The reason is that millions of American women are now entering old age with already weakened skeletons. They haven't yet experienced fractures, but many of them are certain to do so. What is worse, even more millions of young women are failing to take the simple steps that would help them build strong skeletons while they still have the chance. And so for them, forty to fifty years later, the osteoporosis problem may be far worse than it is for today's elderly. There *are* things they—and you—can do to build a strong skeleton, or at least to reduce the chances of suffering an osteoporotic fracture. Waiting until your skeleton is already weakened before taking corrective action is bound to be less effective than keeping your skeleton strong in the first place.

So osteoporosis, bone health, and calcium nutrition are topics every woman needs to know more about. You personally need to know because, while there is much that science still must learn about these matters, there are things you can and should be doing now, steps that will help you have a stronger skeleton and reduce your chances of osteoporotic fractures. There are also steps you can take to reduce the risk for your aging parents or relatives, and things you can do to help your daughters establish lifetime habits that will enhance their chances of having strong skeletons.

You need this information for other reasons, too. We are in the middle of a phenomenon that has been called "the calcium craze." You have been bombarded with signs of it in the media for the last few years. Pharmaceutical manufacturers have marketed dozens of new calcium supplements. Food processing corporations are adding calcium to everything from flour to breakfast cereal. Are these good ideas? Do they work? What are the dangers? Countless articles touting the benefits of calcium have been written. Some experts say you need more calcium. Others say you don't. What or whom can you believe?

The truth is that bone health is too complicated to be reduced to a single issue. While getting enough calcium *is* important, bone health is more than just a matter of getting enough calcium. Calcium can help, but it can't do it all. This book tells you what medical science knows—and doesn't know—about bone health. But equally important, it gives you a firm background of the science involved without requiring specialized training. This book will help you to read the news stories critically, to understand some of the reasons for controversy when it occurs, and to know what questions to ask, both of new products and of your own physicians.

In writing this book we have set out to answer the many questions we have received personally from both the public and from science writers and reporters. If you wonder why we explain how blood calcium levels are regulated, or how vitamin D works, the answer is because people have asked us these questions, or because other questions they have asked could only be answered if first they understood something about these matters. But if such things don't interest you, skip over those chapters. Go to any chapter you want. If you need background knowledge for that chapter, we will tell you where we talked about it earlier. Or check the index.

We have organized the book into five sections. The first is about calcium and bone—what calcium is, where it comes from, how and why it is important for life, and how all higher animals go about regulating their body calcium levels. We also tell you about bone—what it is composed of, how it is constantly being renewed and repaired, how that repair process gets mixed up with our bodies' regulation of calcium levels, and what the forces are that influence how much bone we have at various times in our lives.

The second section is all about calcium nutrition—how much calcium various foods contain, how much our bodies need at various times in our lives, how other factors in our diet may alter our calcium needs, why one person needs more calcium than another, and what the natural calcium intake for humans probably is.

The third section is about illnesses caused by too little calcium in the diet, mainly osteoporosis. But we also talk about high blood pressure and cancer, two disorders that have recently been linked to calcium deficiency. In this section we also discuss dental problems related to diet calcium and we describe the relation between exercise and bone health, with particular emphasis on the problems of young women who are performance athletes. We cover, too, the important consequences for bone of the eating disorders that have reached epidemic proportions in recent years.

In the fourth section we offer practical advice about your calcium intake. We tell you how to estimate your daily calcium needs, and how to get more calcium in your diet. We describe and compare calcium supplements and discuss whether or when they should be used. We talk also about whether calcium is safe and about the growing trend to fortify various natural foods with calcium.

The last part gives practical advice on osteoporosis. We talk about who is at risk. We discuss whether you should have your bones measured in one of the osteoporosis diagnostic centers—what you can and cannot get out of such an experience—and how you can avoid being exploited by purveyors of this new technology. We pull together some of the suggestions scattered throughout the rest of the book in three chapters—one for women who already have osteoporosis, one for parents who want to help their daughters form good health habits and build the strongest possible skeletons while they still have the push of growth to help the process along, and one for the adult children of elderly mothers, who may already have osteoporosis or who are at least at risk. We tell you how you can help them reduce the risk of fracture, or cope with osteoporosis if it is already apparent.

Finally we have appended a glossary, to help you with some of the jargon. And then there is a list of supplemental resources—including, for example, some of the major governmental studies we cite, the names of organizations you can contact for more information, additional readings for those who want to go into some of these topics in greater depth, and even some computer software that you can buy to help you assess your diet. There is also an appendix in which we present some of the background science necessary to understand the points we make in the body of the book. You won't need to read it to follow the outline of our story. But it may answer some of the questions that occur to you as you read some of the chapters in the section on calcium and bones.

CALCIUM AND BONES

2
Calcium in Our Bodies

Calcium, a chemical element, is abundant in rocks, in soil, in rivers, streams, lakes, and the sea. It is found in all plants and animals—in fact, a calcium-free environment would be lifeless. In the human body, as well as in all higher animals, calcium exists in three places: in the skeleton, in the cells, and in the fluids that surround and bathe all body tissues.

Calcium is the stuff of marble, coral, pearls, seashells, eggshells, teeth, chalk, plaster, and, most important for our purposes, bones. In fact, calcium is the fifth most common of the ninety-two chemical elements in the earth's crust.

Calcium is also found in all animals and plants—in fact, life as we know it depends on having calcium in the environment. When life first evolved, it built on and incorporated the calcium that was everywhere, and ever since then there has been an intimate partnership between calcium and the molecules of life.

WHERE CALCIUM IS LOCATED

An adult woman has about 800–900 grams (1.75–2 pounds) of calcium in her body and an adult man, 1,000–1,200 grams (2.25–2.5 pounds). The calcium is in three places:

- 99 percent is in our skeletons, as a component of bone mineral
- 7–8 grams is in our cells, as the trigger for most cell activity

- 1 gram is in the fluids and blood that surround and bathe all of our body tissues (called extracellular fluid —ECF), where its concentration is vital to cell-to-cell communication

In this book, we'll be focusing on the calcium in the skeleton, and on how the amount of calcium in our diets affects it. But the other two roles of calcium are even more crucial to our bodies, and one of them is very much connected to the strength of our bones.

WHERE THE CALCIUM IS

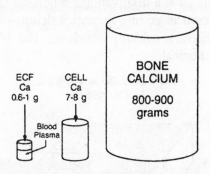

The amount of calcium in our diets has no effect on the amount of calcium in our cells or in our body fluids. Because calcium is essential for cells to survive, they don't rely upon being supplied from the outside, nor do they share their calcium with other cells. Medicine does not yet recognize any disease which alters this within-cell calcium.

CONTROL OF CALCIUM IN THE EXTRACELLULAR FLUID

Our bodies also rigidly regulate the level of calcium in the internal fluids. The drawing (p. 10) shows the location of this fluid, both within the blood and in the little bit of space between all the cells. There is a lot of this extracellular fluid in the body; about 15 percent of body weight is accounted for by this liquid that pervades all our tissues and organs. The body goes to great lengths to regulate the level of calcium and of many other critical elements in this internal sea. The calcium control system is complicated and has numerous backups. If the system fails for any reason, and the level of calcium dissolved in our body fluid gets very far outside a narrow normal range, we get serious symptoms and could easily die.

This control system is important because it allows us to be independent of dietary variations. But the very efficiency of the system puts us at a disadvantage when we try to find out whether a person is getting enough calcium—because even with severe dietary calcium deficiency the blood calcium levels remain normal.

ANATOMY OF A TYPICAL BODY TISSUE

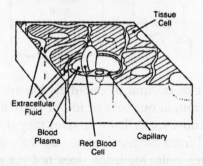

This is because *our bodies use our skeletons not just as mechanical parts, but as a reservoir of calcium*—a place where we can put a little extra calcium if we take in more than we need today, and a place where we can get a little extra, if our diet is deficient today. In fact, many biologists believe that the basic role of bone is not as a structure or support, but as a reservoir of calcium and phosphorus. If there is a loss of calcium from the critical extracellular fluid, the body will tear down bone to use its calcium, and will continue doing this if necessary until the bone is so weak that it can no longer support the body.

Thus the extracellular fluid, which contains only 0.1 percent of all the calcium in the body, is the dominant influence on the skeleton, which contains about 99 percent of the body's calcium.

CALCIUM LOSS AND REPLACEMENT

Although living cells manage to hang on to their calcium very well, still we lose calcium from our bodies every day. This is partly because cells themselves are lost. Old dead skin sloughs off. Hair and nails, consisting of dried-up cells and containing calcium, are formed. The entire lining of the intestine is replaced, at least in the active portions, about once every five days. Those cells are shed into the interior of the intestine where they are digested. Some of their calcium is recovered, but inevitably some is lost in the feces. Sweat also contains calcium, as do the digestive juices and intestinal secretions such as saliva, bile, and mucus produced in the colon. In addition, semen, tears, menstrual flow, and nasal mucus all contain some calcium, and there are further losses through pregnancy and lactation. Finally, urine contains calcium in substantial though varying amounts.

The calcium lost in urine and in the various secretions comes from that critical one gram contained in the extracellular fluid. The new cells formed each day to replace lost skin and intestinal lining and to continue the growth of hair and nails must also get their calcium from the same extracellular fluid. This calcium loss, and the corresponding drain on the extracellular fluid calcium, constitutes something called the obligatory loss. It is likely that, under conditions of extreme privation, the body can reduce obligatory loss to about 100 milligrams (mg) a day. But for most white women in the United States and northern Europe, the figure is closer to 150–200 milligrams. In other words, 15–20 percent of the critical one gram of calcium in the extracellular fluid compartment is irretrievably lost each day. It must be replaced.

The size of this daily calcium loss might surprise you. How did organisms manage to survive with daily loss of such a large proportion of a critical element? For most animals environmental calcium is plentiful. The level of calcium in seawater today is eight to ten times higher than in the extracellular fluid water of fish and all higher animals. So for most marine animals, the problem is not where to get the calcium needed to replace losses, but how to keep from getting too much. For land-living animals, the natural source of calcium is what they eat and drink. For example, a dairy cow gets all she needs not only to build her own skeleton, but also to produce calcium-rich milk. Deer, elk, and caribou get enough to make disposable antlers every year. And they do this by eating grass! They have to eat it nearly all day long, but they get enough.

If, however, animals fail to get enough calcium from their diets, then their systems get the calcium they need from the internal reserve, the skeleton. As we shall see, the mechanisms for doing so are very powerful. The body simply will not tolerate a lowering of the concentration of calcium in that critical extracellular fluid compartment.

Calcium deficiency has not been a common problem in the animal kingdom. Only humans regularly fail to eat a diet sufficient to replace the minimum obligatory calcium loss. The fact that calcium is generally abundant has, in fact, led to relatively poor absorption of calcium from food in many animals. While getting other nutrients from what they ate, most animals have ended up with more calcium than they needed.

Civilized humans are the first animals to eat a relatively calcium-poor diet. Unfortunately, however, we have a digestive system adapted over millennia to deal with surplus, not with deficiency. This, in a nutshell, is why calcium is a problem today.

NOTE: *If you would like to know more about the fascinating relationship between calcium and life, please turn to the appendix at the end of the book.*

3

How Your Body Regulates the Level of Calcium

The amount of calcium in our diets affects how much bone we have, but it has virtually no effect on the amount of calcium in our cells or in our body fluids. This is because calcium is so important for life that human beings—and all higher animals—rigidly regulate the level in the internal body fluids. For this we have evolved a complicated control system with many backups. Even during severe dietary calcium deficiency, the blood calcium levels remain entirely normal. This is because our bodies use our skeletons not just as mechanical parts, but as a reservoir of calcium.

The body regulates the calcium level in the extracellular fluid like a dam regulates a stream. It does it in three ways:

- The kidneys, acting like the dam, can raise or lower the amount of calcium that leaves the body in the urine, within certain limits.
- The body can't control how much calcium we eat, but it can adjust the efficiency of calcium absorption from a low of 10–15 percent of the calcium we ingest to 75–80 percent. (However, this adjustment can work only if the food in the intestine contains enough calcium to make a difference, so what we choose to eat is still important.)
- The body can take care of a calcium surplus by building up bone, and make up for a deficiency by tearing

down bone. Since bone contains calcium in a very concentrated form, building even a little extra bone allows us easily to store a dietary surplus; conversely,
tearing down a little extra bone allows us to keep calcium levels in the body fluids constant.

The body activates these processes with chemical messengers called hormones. Three principal hormones are involved in the calcium-regulating system: parathyroid hormone, calcitonin, and calcitriol.

Parathyroid hormone (PTH for short) is a very small protein
molecule, produced by four tiny glands located in the neck
behind the thyroid gland. They monitor the level of calcium
in the extracellular fluid by checking on the extracellular fluid
in their immediate locale. They quickly release PTH whenever the calcium level falls below the acceptable range. Individuals who have lost the capacity to make PTH (because of
surgical removal of the parathyroid glands, or because of
damage incurred during thyroid surgery) cannot regulate extracellular fluid calcium. Their ECF calcium levels are low,
which produces symptoms such as muscle spasms and rigidity.
The purpose of PTH is to keep the level of calcium in the
extracellular fluid up to normal. We will describe how PTH
does this in a moment.

Calcitonin, like PTH, is a very small protein. It is called into
action whenever the level of calcium gets too high.
Calcitonin is produced by cells embedded within the thyroid
gland. Calcitonin seems to be most important during infancy,
when a lot of calcium enters the system from milk. Adults
who are unable to make calcitonin (because of surgical removal of the thyroid) do not seem to have any trouble regulating their extracellular fluid calcium levels. Thus, in adults
calcitonin is probably not important. How calcitonin works,
we shall see in a moment.

Calcitriol is the active form of the substance we have for
years called vitamin D. Calcitriol is the most recently discovered of the calcium-regulating hormones, and its effects are

not yet all understood. Calcitriol is produced in the kidney in response to stimulation by PTH, and increases absorption of dietary calcium in the intestine, among other effects. In the intestine it causes the cells lining the small bowel to make a special transport protein that binds calcium reversibly and shuttles it through the intestinal lining to the bloodstream. It was once commonly held that vitamin D is necessary for absorption of calcium from food. We now know that that is only partly true. We can absorb calcium in the total absence of calcitriol (or of other members of the vitamin D family), but not efficiently. If we regularly ate diets containing very large quantities of calcium, we probably would need very little calcitriol and we would make very little. But if we are to adapt to low calcium intakes, we must have calcitriol to increase calcium absorption efficiency.

Now that we know the principal actors—the hormones—we can link them to the processes they regulate, and roughly outline how the system works.

HOW THE CONTROL SYSTEM OPERATES

Whenever levels of calcium in the extracellular fluid drop below acceptable levels, the parathyroid glands swing into action and produce PTH, which is carried quickly by the bloodstream to its target tissues. In the kidney PTH quickly raises the threshold for calcium excretion. So it shuts down calcium loss in the urine. This stops further urinary loss, but by itself that would mean little if there were no calcium inflow into the system. So PTH sees to this as well, by acting on the bone remodeling apparatus. PTH increases the amount of bone destruction. (We will see the details later.) Thus it quickly increases the inflow of calcium into the extracellular fluid by tapping the skeletal reserve. This increased inflow of calcium complements the effect of the elevated kidney threshold. But PTH doesn't stop there. As we have seen, PTH is also the signal that causes certain cells in the kidney to produce calcitriol, increasing the absorption of calcium from the diet.

The mechanisms that have evolved for dealing with the other extreme—too much calcium—are weaker than the powerful system just described. When the calcium level in the extracellular fluid is too high, calcitonin produces a temporary suppression of bone destruction, thus reducing inflow of calcium into the system. This is particularly important while an infant is absorbing calcium from a milk feeding. The amount of calcium contained in an ordinary feeding is potentially enough to produce a dangerously high calcium level. And yet absorption must be efficient, because infants need calcium to sustain growth. Bone is an extremely active organ in infants and young children. It is growing and reshaping at a prodigious rate, and that process involves bone destruction as well as bone formation. New bone formation can soak up —in fact needs—all the calcium it can get from the feeding. But it cannot handle calcium as fast as the combined inflow from bone destruction and dietary absorption provides. So calcitonin temporarily reduces bone destruction to compensate for the intermittently high calcium inflow from the diet.

You can now see how bone is used as a reservoir, a place to store excess calcium and a place to get needed calcium. This primitive function of the skeleton explains why calcium deficiency in adults may lead to serious skeletal problems.

4
Calcium and Your Bones

Bone is made of a dense network of protein fiber bundles arranged in layers like plywood. In these bundles there are dense accumulations of mineral crystals—calcium phosphate. Bone is a marvelous engineering structure. The protein fibers make bone strong and flexible, and the crystals make it hard. Calcium makes up about 20–25 percent of the weight of bone.

Bone is built of a dense network of fibers made up mainly of a protein called collagen. The fibers are extremely long protein chains coiled around one another, like heavy rope or steel cable. In bone these fibers are arranged in alternating layers like plywood. In the crevices of these fibers are tiny crystals of calcium salts—mainly a type of calcium phosphate called hydroxyapatite, but there is also a certain amount of calcium carbonate. Calcium makes up about 20–25 percent of the weight of bone. The physical properties of bone are the result of a complex interaction between the pliable protein fibers and the hard mineral crystals. The protein fibers make the bone strong and flexible, and the crystals make it hard.

The fine structures of bone are arranged in an efficient architectural pattern that produces the greatest strength and rigidity with the least material. As the drawing shows, each long bone—like those in the arms, legs, hands, and feet—consists of a hollow, tubular shaft with solid walls, much like a piece of pipe. Covering the ends are three-dimensional lattices of thin bony plates intersecting with one another and spreading out to support the surfaces of the joints. The dense

BONE ARCHITECTURE

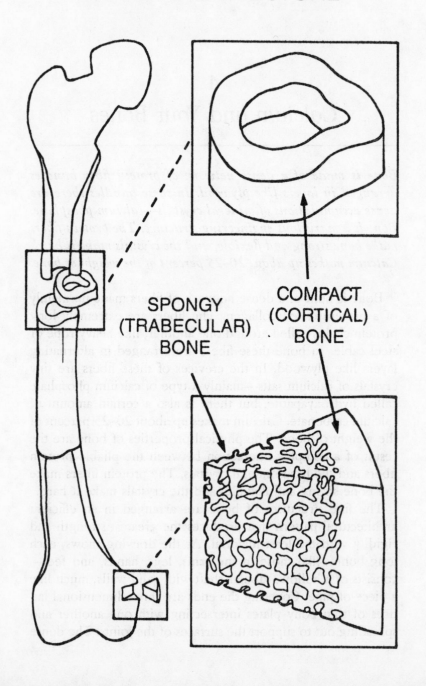

SPONGY
(TRABECULAR)
BONE

COMPACT
(CORTICAL)
BONE

bone of the shaft is called cortical bone. The latticelike bone at the ends is called cancellous or trabecular bone, and the plates within this kind of bone are called trabeculae.

Other bones, including the vertebrae (spine) and pelvis, have a thin skin of cortical bone and an interior filled with trabecular bone also arranged in a honeycomb of intersecting plates. The weight of the body is carried by the vertical trabeculae. But by themselves these are not massive enough to withstand very much force. Horizontal trabeculae act as cross-braces to prevent buckling of the vertical plates, thereby providing great strength with as little mass as possible. It is a beautifully constructed structural system.

OSTEOCYTES IN BONE

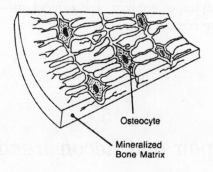

Osteocyte

Mineralized
Bone Matrix

Dense and hard as bone is, even the thin bony plates are not entirely solid. The living cells that make up 4 percent of bone's volume are evenly distributed throughout (see drawing). Even though they comprise only a very small fraction of bone volume, bone cells are extremely important. Because these living cells need to be supplied with oxygen and energy, they need contact with the bloodstream. So a network of tiny blood vessels runs all through bone. The cells, isolated within the bony substance, nevertheless maintain contact with one another, and ultimately with the blood vessel nourishing a group of them, through a network of tiny tunnels running all through the bone. The protoplasm of these bone cells extends through these tunnels. Each bone cell is like a tiny octopus with tentacles extending throughout its immediate neighborhood.

The cells buried in bone are called osteocytes. They were originally bone-forming cells (called osteoblasts), but, in the process of making new bone, they have walled themselves in. They continue to live in the interior, no longer making bone, but serving another crucial function that we shall describe later.

The inside and outside surfaces of bone are covered with a layer of living cells that are inactive most of the time, but can become osteoblasts and form new bone. Also found in bones, at least at sites of active bone destruction, are giant cells that eat into bone surfaces. They are called osteoclasts. These three—osteocytes, osteoblasts, and osteoclasts—are principal actors in bone remodeling.

5

Repair and Reconstruction

Although bone is strong and somewhat flexible, normal wear and tear causes microscopic cracks or defects. These are repaired in an ongoing process called bone remodeling in which bone is first torn down and then built up. Bone remodeling is carried out almost exactly like structural remodeling of our homes and workplaces. It is organized into small individual projects that are carried out by specialized cells.

The remodeling of bones is continuous. In adults, from 6 to 12 percent of the total skeleton is replaced every year. If remodeling were spread evenly throughout the skeleton (which it's not), an individual would create a completely new skeleton once every eight to sixteen years. Children and young adults remodel much more rapidly than adults.

Bone remodeling is quite similar to remodeling of a building. The reasons are similar, too. There has been some damage, and we need to replace the damaged material; or we're putting the part to a different use, and we need to reshape it to serve that purpose better. "Steps in Bone Remodeling" (p. 22) illustrates the steps in this important activity. Panel A depicts a microscopic block of bone with inactive lining cells on its surface. A small area of microdamage is indicated.

DEMOLITION

In remodeling a building, workers first remove damaged material. In bone (Panel B), this job is done by specialized cells called osteoclasts. Removal of old bone must precede its replacement by new bone.

NEW CONSTRUCTION

After the bone has been cleared away, the osteoclasts somehow sense that their job is done, and they withdraw from the worksite, leaving behind a clean excavation (Panel C) or sometimes even a tunnel. Under normal circumstances the osteoclasts are followed very rapidly by osteoblasts that move in and begin to lay down new bone (Panel D). They first manufacture the collagen fibers that make up the matrix of bone. They lay these fibers down on the freshly excavated surface and orient them to give the new bone strength in the directions in which it is likely to be stressed.

STEPS IN BONE REMODELING

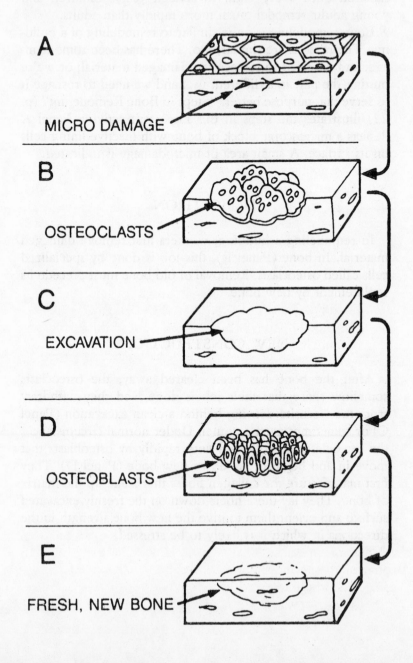

A

MICRO DAMAGE

B

OSTEOCLASTS

C

EXCAVATION

D

OSTEOBLASTS

E

FRESH, NEW BONE

Mineralization

At this point the new bone is only protein matrix or network, about half protein and half water. (That's still dense, as body tissues go. Meat, which we think of as a particularly protein-rich tissue, is about one fifth protein and four fifths water.) The osteoblasts then produce certain specialized enzymes which they leave behind to work on the protein matrix. These enzymes convert a portion of the fiber structures to a configuration that traps calcium and phosphorus, thereby causing the whole structure to calcify in about ten days. As mineral accumulates, it displaces water. When calcification is complete, all the water has been displaced and all the space used up by the protein and the mineral which encrusts it (Panel E). By the time calcification occurs, the osteoblasts have moved some distance away from the calcifying site. During that time they have deposited more layers of protein matrix, each of which will, in turn, calcify about ten days after it has been formed.

The building blocks of bone mineral are literally sucked out of the blood by the growing crystals. Bone, fully mineralized, contains eight hundred times as much calcium as an equal volume of extracellular fluid! In this way newly forming bone is one of the main outflows of calcium from the extracellular fluid. In fact, in adult women it comprises about two thirds of the total calcium outflow from the system. (See "The Daily Ins and Outs of Calcium" on page 24.)

ORGANIZATION OF REMODELING

Bone remodeling is organized into small, individual projects. About 5–10 percent of bone is undergoing remodeling at any time. And as in buildings, remodeling is generally confined to specific sites. In bone something must tell the osteoclasts where to do their destructive work and how far to go. No one yet knows what the activation signal is. Never-

THE DAILY INS AND OUTS
OF CALCIUM (mg)

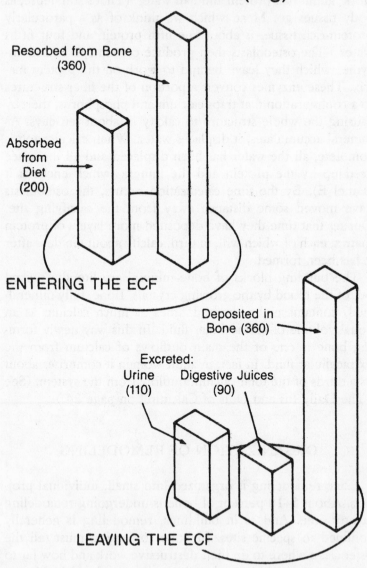

Resorbed from Bone
(360)

Absorbed
from
Diet
(200)

ENTERING THE ECF

Deposited in
Bone (360)

Excreted:
Urine   Digestive Juices
(110)   (90)

LEAVING THE ECF

Why Bones Calcify and Other Tissues Don't

All connective tissues, not just bone, contain bundles of collagen fibers. But normally only bone calcifies. The reason is that the cells that lay down the fibers in other connective tissues do not take the second step of producing enzymes that alter the protein so that it will trap calcium. This second step—unique to osteoblasts—allows calcification of new bone to be sustained by levels of calcium in the extracellular fluid which do not tend to precipitate elsewhere. This is part of the reason why we normally calcify bone and teeth, but not other tissues.

The other part is found in a unique feature of the calcium salt found in bone. The same *chemical* substance can have very different *physical* properties when its constituent atoms are arranged in different patterns. The principal mineral of bone, as we have noted, is a compound of calcium and phosphate called hydroxyapatite. It will not spontaneously form except under special conditions. And the enzymes out there in that ten-day-old protein matrix of new bone create these special conditions. No one knows exactly how it happens, but the result is clear. Once a tiny crystal of hydroxyapatite begins to form, it grows until it runs out of room to expand further. The concentrations of calcium and phosphorus in the extracellular fluid are more than sufficient to support the growth of hydroxyapatite crystals. Those same calcium concentrations do not lead to calcification elsewhere because the conditions required for calcification normally exist only in newly forming bone. Thus bones, but not other tissues, calcify, even though all are bathed by the same extracellular fluid, and all are exposed to the same levels of calcium and phosphorus.

theless, the remodeling process works. The sequence of activation, destruction, and repair happens at a microscopic level,
too small to be seen with the naked eye, and generally invisible to X rays as well. Each remodeling unit in a normal adult
removes and replaces about 0.1 cubic millimeter of bone.
That's only one tenth the volume occupied by the head of a
pin. There are nearly one million of these tiny remodeling
jobs going on in an adult skeleton at any time. In mature
adults the process takes about three to six months. As people
age, the process takes longer and longer, and in skeletons of
old persons, there is often evidence of incomplete work. The
workers seem to have quit before the job was done. Either
the osteoblasts failed to move in to fill the excavation left by
the osteoclasts or they stopped before restoring all of the
excavated bone. We are not certain why.

We noted at the beginning of this chapter that the purposes
of remodeling in bone and remodeling in homes and buildings are similar—to replace damaged material or to recon-
figure the structure for new purposes. In our homes and of-
fices damaged material and new uses mean a water pipe has
burst, or there has been a small fire, or a tree limb has fallen
onto the roof, or a window frame has rotted. The damage
must be fixed if the building is not to fall apart and become
unusable. But what does damage mean in terms of bone?

REPAIR OF DAMAGED BONE

Bone is strong and somewhat flexible, but there are limits.
Even in normal use microscopic cracks or defects appear in
the bony material. The layers of mineral-encrusted collagen
fibers pull apart, fibers are torn. This wear and tear is too
small to see with the naked eye or even with X rays, and it is
very hard to demonstrate, even under a microscope. But special methods used by materials scientists show that it's there.
It's similar to the metal fatigue that occurs in airplane wings,
jet engine supports, and bridge bolts. Once such defects de-

velop, they tend to get worse, just as a tear in a piece of fabric gets worse unless it is quickly repaired.

This is where the osteocytes—the living bone cells—come into the picture. They seem to be the damage detection system of bone. Fatigue cracks in the bony material come into contact with the octopus network of osteocyte cells running all through the extracellular material of bone. When bone is bent or deformed—as always happens to some extent when we work or exercise—tiny electrical charges arise in the material in much the same way that the vibration of the needle of a phonograph cartridge evokes small electrical signals which are amplified to make music. This is happening all the time in most of our bones—even during sleep, for even then muscles are pulling and tugging at the bones. So there is a constant shifting background of electrical activity in the bones, and the osteocytes are accustomed to it. But when even the tiniest crack develops, bending and shearing forces tend to concentrate there, simply because it is a point where the structure tends to "give" more easily. This exaggerated electrical activity around the crack indicates the presence of a defect and alerts the osteocytes to the presence of local damage.

What happens next isn't known in detail. The osteocytes seem to transmit a damage signal, passing the message on to one another through the tunnels that run all through the bone, until it reaches the lining cells on a free surface where the blood vessels lie. There, if enough osteocytes have sent in a signal, a remodeling site is activated. Cells carried to the site by the blood are transformed into osteoclasts, and they excavate inward in the direction of the signal, all the way to the defect.

It seems likely also that the osteocytes are able to make temporary, makeshift repairs of their own—perhaps like spackling the cracks in a plaster wall. Such temporary repairs don't solve the basic problem, but they may keep the defect from spreading rapidly.

MATERIAL DEFECTS AND BONE STRENGTH/
WEAKNESS

If tiny wear-and-tear defects are not continuously removed and replaced with fresh new bone, fractures will occur, even in bone that looks normal. Small defects, left untended, get bigger and bigger with no more stress than that produced by everyday activity. Then at some point a very minor fall or injury results in a complete break.

There are at least two circumstances in which this type of fracture occurs. The first is in bone that has been damaged by therapeutic radiation, as for the treatment of cancer of an organ in the vicinity of a bone. The radiation kills or impairs the bone cells, either those involved in detecting damage or those that react to it, perhaps both. Even though the bone usually appears quite normal on X rays, invisible fatigue cracks grow and extend until a complete break occurs. Here the problem occurs because of impairment of the damage-control apparatus in bone. Another circumstance occurs when cracks develop and grow faster than the normal repair process can keep up with them. This can happen when there is a sudden shift from relative inactivity to intense, continuous, hard physical work. New recruits in the armed services sometimes develop fractures in foot bones (called "march fractures") when they are abruptly exposed to intensive marching, drilling, and running.

When a person has thin, light bones—for whatever reason —ordinary work or exercise will result in more bending and twisting of the bones—and thus more microdamage—than would occur if they were heavy and dense. (This doesn't mean that work and exercise should be avoided, as we shall see.) Repair is thus more important when bones are thin than when they are heavy. Thin bone is more fragile than heavier bone. It's not just a question of a less massive structure. Thin bones suffer more fatigue damage, and they need a more active, more vigilant repair mechanism.

6

The Calcium Economy
and Bone Remodeling

---

*Our bodies do not store calcium simply as a chemical element;
they store it as bone. Since bone contains calcium in a very
concentrated form, building up even a little bone allows us
easily to store a dietary surplus. Conversely, tearing down a
little bone releases a lot of calcium to keep calcium levels in
the body fluids constant.*

There is a fascinating consequence of the sequence of destruction first, then repair, that characterizes bone remodeling. At any site, remodeling first makes calcium available to
the rest of the body and then later takes it back. While some
sites are destroying bone, others are forming it. Thus, on
average, our skeleton demands about as much calcium as it
liberates.

Remodeling adds to, and takes from, the extracellular fluid
compartment a quantity of calcium greater than the corresponding flows provided by diet and excretion (See "The
Daily Ins and Outs of Calcium", p. 24). So anything that gets
bone destruction and bone formation out of phase—even
temporarily—could easily result in major changes in extracellular fluid calcium concentrations. The system responsible for
keeping those levels constant has had to contend with this
problem.

REMODELING AS A WAY OF ADJUSTING BODY CALCIUM LEVELS

But a problem might actually be an opportunity! And so this one turns out to be. Deliberately getting bone destruction and formation out of phase is a fine way to make calcium temporarily available when the extracellular fluid compartment is short of calcium, or to soak up the excess when the extracellular fluid compartment has too much. We have already seen that, during absorption of calcium from an infant feeding, calcitonin suppresses bone destruction temporarily. We have also seen that when the extracellular fluid calcium level falls, PTH increases bone destruction. We can now recognize that these changes are simply a fine-tuning of the bone remodeling system, and we begin to get a glimmer of how the calcium economy is integrated with the bone remodeling process.

If the bone remodeling apparatus gets a strong enough signal that there is damage somewhere, it will activate a remodeling site. It turns out that the hormone PTH, which we have seen is the principal factor conserving calcium for our internal needs and keeping our extracellular fluid calcium up to normal levels, also determines the responsiveness of the bone remodeling apparatus to signals indicating damage. When PTH levels rise, the remodeling apparatus becomes more responsive, and more remodeling sites are activated. That immediately makes more calcium available, for the first stage of remodeling is the destructive stage, in which bone is torn down and its constituents are released into the blood.

A fine example of the integration of these two systems is played out every spring when deer form new antlers. Antlers are bone, and their rapid formation creates a huge demand for calcium. Winter is a time of relative starvation, and the scant winter and early spring fodder available to the deer do not contain sufficient calcium to meet this suddenly increased demand. So the deer crank up the bone remodeling apparatus, perhaps taking care of a backlog of bone repair projects that might have been deferred all winter. This occurs through increased production of PTH, an increase that is evoked by the tendency of the extracellular fluid calcium level to fall as newly forming antlers take up calcium. As we have noted, a sudden increase in remodeling makes abundant calcium available, since all of the newly activated sites are in the destructive—or calcium-releasing—phase of remodeling. Weeks later, after the antlers are fully formed, those remodeling sites will have progressed naturally into the bone-forming stages. By then, rich summer grasses and foliage are available, and the deer can get all the calcium they need from food. This whole process illustrates how beautifully the system fits together. But it also underscores the abundance of calcium in the environment of most animals. For each year the deer throw away all this calcium as they shed their antlers. For them, getting enough calcium is not the problem. It is primarily a matter of timing.

REMODELING AND CALCIUM DEFICIENCY

But in other circumstances, the usual response of the remodeling apparatus to the need for calcium may not be so innocuous. For example, put laboratory animals on a calcium-restricted diet. The need here is not to make antlers but to replace the animal's minimum obligatory loss, which would otherwise lead to a fall in the calcium level of the extracellular fluid. Extra remodeling sites are activated to provide calcium. But, as with deer, the remodeling sites activated to provide calcium will inexorably move into their own bone-formation phase and thereby create their own demand for calcium. This forces the parathyroid glands to even higher activity. More PTH is released, and more and more bone remodeling is activated, always in an attempt to provide enough calcium to meet the combined demands both of minimum obligatory loss and of remodeling sites previously activated to make their calcium available, but now in the bone-forming, calcium-demanding stage of remodeling. The system can't keep up, of course, for there is daily loss of calcium out of the body. If that loss is not replaced through diet, accelerated bone remodeling inevitably results in net bone destruction. Some animals, such as cats, which are normally accustomed to very high calcium diets, cannot reduce their minimum obligatory loss very effectively when placed on low-calcium diets. They experience rapid bone loss, perhaps as much as a third of their total bone substance in only three or four months. Other animals adapt better, and serious bone loss takes longer, but in all animals the result is ultimately the same.

This condition of reduced bone mass is called osteoporosis, and it is clear from experiments in many different animal species that low-calcium diets can cause it, by exactly the mechanisms just described. But osteoporosis can be caused by many other factors besides calcium deficiency. The details of the role of calcium in osteoporosis will be explored later.

7

How Much Bone Will You Have?

If we are to be strong enough to do hard physical work and to withstand falls and other mishaps, we need heavy skeletons. The amount of bone we have—our bone mass—is influenced by heredity, by nutrition, by work and exercise, and by hormones. When we stop growing, bone mass continues to increase until about age thirty-five. The best protection against future bone problems is to build the best skeleton we can while our bodies are still in a "building mood"—while we are still young.

The amount of bone we have—our bone mass—is influenced by several factors. Their relative importance is reflected in the size of the cubes in the drawing below.

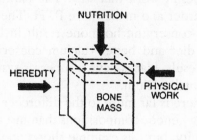

INFLUENCES AFFECTING BONE QUANTITY

Heredity

The most basic influence is heredity. Some of us are destined to have big, heavy bones, and others, light, delicate bones—just as some of us are destined to have straight or curly hair, and blue or brown eyes. Some of these features, like eye color, are fixed from the beginning. Others, like the size and density of adult bones, though present in the genetic blueprint, don't become obvious until growth is nearly finished. But given a healthy childhood, and even marginally adequate nutrition, those of us destined to have big bones will develop them. Those of us destined to have small bones will not get big ones, no matter what we do.

Whites and Asiatics generally have lighter bone structures than blacks of the same height and weight, even during infancy and childhood. And within the many ethnic groups of whites, there is considerable additional variation. We recognize this when we call some persons "big-boned," or when we say others have "delicate features."

We now know some of the ways genes influence bone mas-

siveness. For instance, the bones of blacks are slightly more
resistant to the action of parathyroid hormone (PTH) than
are the bones of whites. We described in Chapter 6 how bone
provides a reserve store of calcium, and how the body draws
on that reserve by PTH-stimulated bone remodeling. So in
blacks bones are less readily torn down to make up for a
shortage of calcium in the extracellular fluid. That might be
bad, if it meant a fall in calcium level in the extracellular
fluid. But it doesn't work that way. The parathyroid glands
simply work harder and make more PTH. The higher levels
of this calcium-conserving hormone result in better absorption from the diet and better calcium conservation by the
kidneys. As a result, blacks have a superior system for utiliz-
ing environmental calcium.

Of course, there is far more to the difference between persons of differing genetic compositions than just this difference
in PTH sensitivity, but this example shows one way in which
genetic programs are translated into physical differences.

Physical Activity

If you have a delicate skeleton, it can't be transformed into
a big-boned one, but you can affect bone massiveness by
physical activity, or exercise, or to put it simply, *work.* Bones
are like muscles: "use 'em or lose 'em!" Each of us has about
as much bone, within genetic limits, as is needed to withstand
the stresses that everyday activity places upon our skeletons.

Other things being equal, the person who does hard physical work all day long will have a heavier skeleton than one
who is sedentary—just as the first person will have strong,
heavy muscles, and the second weak and flabby ones. Athletes have heavier skeletons than do office workers, and
olympic-class athletes have heavier skeletons than do college
athletes. All of this, of course, represents variation around an
individual, genetically programmed level (the dashed lines
indicating variations in the size of the cube in the diagram at
the beginning of this chapter).

On the other hand, persons who are inactive, who are paralyzed, who do little physical work, who are ill and have restricted activity or are even bedfast, and even astronauts—who spend an extended period of time having to do none of the work of resisting gravity—either develop less bone massiveness than they could have, or lose some of what they once had. Anyone who becomes bedfast begins to lose bone from day one.

This kind of bone loss is mostly reversible, perhaps entirely so, at least up to the age of forty or fifty—but only if normal physical activity can be resumed. Studies done at the University of Wisconsin and at Brookhaven National Laboratories have shown that even people in their seventies and eighties can add weight and strength to their bones if they undertake a regular program of appropriate physical exercise. We don't know how much they can add, but it is encouraging that it is never too late.

No one knows what kind of exercise is best. Many experts believe that gravity-resisting exercise is better than other kinds, and they would say, therefore, that swimming would not be as beneficial as other sorts of exercise. We think the evidence for this conclusion is weak. Olympic swimmers are known to have heavier, stronger skeletons than nonathletes. So far as medical science knows, any exercise is better than no exercise, though perhaps some kinds may prove to be more effective than others. For example, the *rate* at which bone is stressed seems to have more effect on bone mass than does simply the *amount* of the stress. Thus, kicking an obstacle away provides more stimulus to bone in the foot and leg than just pushing it away with the foot. And jumping, running, or jogging provides more stimulus than walking the same distance.

It seems likely that the awkwardness of children and young people interacts with their genetic programs to help them build the strongest possible skeletons. Children and adolescents run down the stairs, slam doors, wrench open cupboards, and otherwise wreck the house. Sometimes we despair of their ever becoming graceful—by which we mean performing an action smoothly and with as little force as necessary. But if rate of strain is the important factor, then it is the violent actions that stimulate the skeleton. Ironically, the acquired gracefulness of maturity, in an environment filled with labor-saving devices, removes an important stimulus to maintain bone weight and strength. Even in regular exercise —as in playing tennis—the better player gets less of a workout than the poorer one. There may be consolation in this for klutzes!

Diet

The third factor that determines how massive our bones will be is nutrition—principally the amount of calcium in the diet, but also, as we shall see later, vitamin D, phosphorus, protein, and trace minerals, among others.

The calcium needed to form new bone comes to the bone-forming site from the extracellular fluid, and if bone is to grow, it must take more calcium out of that extracellular fluid than it puts back through the remodeling process. But this can only happen if a person eats a diet rich enough in calcium, and absorbs well enough from that diet, to replace the calcium taken out of the extracellular fluid by bone. It is for this reason that dietary calcium is necessary for our genes to express themselves and for physical activity to build heavier bones. Good nutrition allows these other factors to operate. But an adequate-calcium diet—even a high-calcium diet— will not cause us to have a big skeleton or heavy bones if we're not genetically programmed that way, or if we are not putting our bones to work with physical activity.

NASA demonstrated the relationship of calcium intake and mechanical loading in studies done to simulate the effects of prolonged weightlessness. Healthy male volunteers were subjected to complete bedrest for three to six months. They lost a great deal of bone, mostly from their feet and legs. The heel bone in some of those volunteers, for example, lost as much as 40 percent of its mass over a thirty-week period. (All the lost bone came back when the volunteers started walking

It is not known how exercise affects the skeleton. Probably it has something to do with those electrical fields produced in bone whenever it twists or bends. We saw how a local exaggeration of those electrical fields may be the signal that activates remodeling sites, and we noted that there is a constant background of shifting electrical charges produced by any mechanical stressing of the skeleton.

It appears that there is a certain level of such electrical activity that is just right, that is, a level that keeps the destruction and formation of bone remodeling in balance. If a region of bone is no longer being used, there are no twisting and bending forces acting on it to produce this local electrical activity. Such a region is simply removed by remodeling. Osteoclasts move in and destroy bone, but no osteoblasts follow to replace what was taken out. Or, if osteoblasts do appear, they lay down less bone than was removed. Conversely, a region with a lot of general electrical activity gets remodeled by destroying only a little old bone, and then forming a lot of new bone on the excavated remodeling site. Thus, as the bone grows in size, and the walls and latticework of bone get thicker, the bone gets stronger and bends less and less with daily mechanical stresses. As a result the electrical fields that are caused by bending are correspondingly reduced. In this way the amount of bone we have in any region of our skeletons is continually being adjusted up and down to match the amount of stress we're currently placing on it by the level and type of physical activity we're now doing.

again, so no lasting harm was done.) The NASA researchers tried large calcium supplements, but there was no reduction of the bone loss. That doesn't mean that calcium isn't important—just that it can't work without exercise.

Though sufficient calcium in the diet is not enough by itself, it nevertheless is essential. These volunteers couldn't
have reversed this bone loss when they resumed normal activity if their diets were not adequate in calcium. Or at least,
if they had accomplished some repair, the calcium would
have had to come from bone somewhere else in the skeleton.
They would have had to take a little bone from all over the
skeleton to replace the bone lost from the feet and legs.

We have already noted that most animals lose bone even
without a reduction in activity level if we put them on a
calcium-deficient diet or if we block calcium absorption from
the diet. The same is surely true for humans. Adequate calcium intake *and* absorption are necessary to protect and to
conserve skeletal mass. But, once again, taking more calcium
than we need will not cause our bones to increase in size or
massiveness above levels determined jointly by heredity and
level of use in exercise or work.

So to build as much bone as we are genetically programmed to have, to have as much bone as current physical
activity demands, and to conserve the bone we have already
built, an adequate calcium intake is essential.

BONE MASS AND LIFE STAGES

As one would expect, the amount of bone we have increases throughout infancy, childhood, and adolescence.
However, bone mass does not stop increasing when adult
height is achieved. By age 18, when most of us have stopped
growing taller, our bones are still relatively light, and not as
strong as they are destined to be. The cortex in the shafts of
long bones is thin and somewhat porous, and the trabecular
plates are thin as well. This is partly because growth in length
during the adolescent growth spurt has occurred faster than
the body could take in the calcium needed for full skeletal
mass. Skeletal consolidation continues all through the twen-

ties and into the mid-thirties. Most of us don't reach our peak bone mass until about age thirty-five. During all this time our bodies are striving to finish construction according to the specifications of the genetic blueprint. The best protection against future bone problems is to build the best skeleton we can while our bodies are still in a "building mood"—while we are still young. Women generally have smaller, lighter skeletons than men, even men of the same height and weight. This is due partly to genetic differences, and partly to hormones. Estrogen, the female hormone, suppresses bone remodeling, and so is a potent growth arrester. Further, it limits bone expansion after growth in height has ceased. Girls go through puberty earlier than boys, and thus they stop growing at a younger age.

After age thirty-five bone mass levels off for five to ten years in both men and women, and then begins a slow decline which continues over the rest of the life span. There are many reasons for this decline. One we have already seen—decreased physical activity. We become more graceful or skillful, and we expend less energy in many of our physical activities. At a certain stage of our lives we delegate to our children cutting the grass, spading the garden, shoveling the sidewalk, and other physical chores we used to do for ourselves. We sometimes pay a high cost in exasperation for this "help," but exasperation doesn't stimulate our skeletons; physical work does. Sometimes individuals become more affluent as well, and so use more labor-saving devices or pay someone else to do their physical work. Whatever the reasons, most of us work less hard physically with each year. The skeleton is stressed less and less, and the system responds by adjusting overall bone mass downward to match a new level of use.

Calcium intake falls with age as well, as we shall discuss later in detail. In some people this undoubtedly contributes to the decline in bone mass.

A third reason is what we might call accumulated errors of

aging. For example, while remodeling a trabecular plate, the osteoclasts occasionally erode completely through the full thickness. A hole or window is left, instead of just an excavation. The osteoblasts that move in later to lay down new bone no longer have a complete surface on which to work. So the hole cannot be closed, and some of the bone lost during the destructive phase of remodeling cannot be replaced. Such inevitable, irreversible mistakes accumulate with age, and they contribute to the decline in skeletal mass.

Thus far we have been discussing causes that are common to both men and women. A major difference between the sexes is the natural, abrupt loss of sex hormones that occurs in women at menopause (or earlier, if a woman has had her ovaries removed by surgery). The loss of estrogen has profound effects on a woman's skeleton. There is less resistance to the destructive effects of PTH, and probably to other forces as well. Whatever the mechanism, when a woman loses estrogen, she very rapidly loses bone as well. Some bony regions appear to be more sensitive than others—the spine, for example. But, averaged over the whole skeleton, a woman will lose from 10 to 15 percent of her total bone mass in the first ten years after menopause. The same kind of bone loss occurs whether a woman loses estrogen at age twenty-five or age fifty. Scientists disagree about the explanation, but the fact of estrogen protection of the skeleton is not in dispute.

The rate of bone loss after estrogen deprivation is fastest in the first two to three years and gradually slows until, by age sixty-five or seventy, a woman is losing bone mass at only the same slow rate of a man her age. But in those intervening years, from about age fifty to seventy, she will have lost perhaps 25 percent of the bone she had at menopause. For some women, the loss in the spine can be even greater.

Prompt replacement of estrogen in menopausal women will completely prevent that bone loss. However, the decision to take estrogen after menopause is a complicated one.

Estrogen replacement therapy (ERT) involves potential risks as well as benefits for many different organ systems, not just bone. We cover the subject in detail in chapter 31.

It may well be that if nutrition, physical activity, and other life-style factors were optimum throughout life, the bone loss associated with menopause could be endured without hazard. But conditions are often far from optimum. We neither advocate nor decry estrogen use for every woman. But estrogen is by far the most effective agent known for averting the bone loss that otherwise occurs in all women following menopause.

PUTTING IT ALL TOGETHER

We can best summarize the factors that influence bone mass by diagramming the bone lifeline of a typical white, North American female. (See "Bone Lifeline.")

Bone mass increases rapidly through adolescence, then more slowly till age thirty-five. It then plateaus and begins to decline, then plummets rapidly after menopause until, by age sixty-five, it is getting close to the danger zone in which bones can break with little or no trauma. Of course, some women will be below the average line all their lives, and they will get into the danger zone for fractures sooner. Others, with more bone mass, may never get into that zone.

Every woman follows her own bone lifeline. There are times when she can influence its direction and course, and times when she cannot. Genetics dominates the picture early in life, and she can't do much about that. And toward the end of life there are the accumulated errors of aging, also beyond our control. Physical work and exercise are very important, particularly following menopause. Calcium intake is important throughout life also, though for different reasons at different stages of life. Both exercise and nutrition are under your control. These are things you *can* do something about.

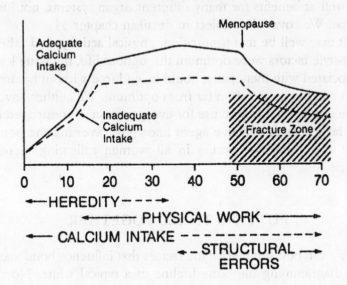

BONE LIFELINE

Menopause

Adequate
Calcium
Intake

Inadequate
Calcium
Intake

Fracture Zone

0   10   20   30   40   50   60   70

←—HEREDITY ---→

←————— PHYSICAL WORK ————→

←—— CALCIUM INTAKE ——————→

←— STRUCTURAL ——→
ERRORS

8

The Vitamin D Story

Vitamin D is essential for the healthy functioning of many steps in the calcium economy. We used to think it was necessary only for calcium absorption. We now know that calcium can be absorbed without vitamin D, but not very efficiently. You need vitamin D to be able to adapt to low calcium intake. You need it to tap skeletal reserves of calcium and to increase the efficiency of calcium absorption from your diet. The natural way to get vitamin D is through exposure to sunlight.

The substance we call vitamin D is an important part of the calcium regulatory system. Individuals who do not get enough vitamin D must have very calcium-rich diets, because without vitamin D they cannot adjust to low or even average calcium intakes. And if they don't adjust, then, as we have seen, they will slowly but surely tear down their own skeletons in order to scavenge the calcium contained in the resulting debris.

Vitamin D, the vitamin of most importance to the calcium story, is the odd member of the vitamin family. It is not normally present in the diet either of humans or of most animals; it does not function as the business end of an enzyme, as do most vitamins; and unlike the others, we can easily make all we need for ourselves. So how did it get to be called a vitamin? By mistake, actually. It was grouped with the other, *real* vitamins early in the century, when it was found that something added to the diet could prevent a bone disease called rickets. So it was assumed that vitamin D was something that should have been in food, but had been removed in processing, or cooking (as polishing rice had removed its thiamine, leading to beriberi).

In the disease called rickets, the complex cellular apparatus that produces growth at the ends of the long bones fails to mineralize, and the levels of calcium and phosphorus—especially phosphorus—in the extracellular fluid are low. As a result, there is impaired bone growth, with bowed legs and bony deformities, particularly around the joints. About a century ago at least 80 percent of the children in the cities of northern and central Europe suffered from this disorder. However, children living by the sea and eating fish did not get rickets, and it was ultimately found that adding fish oils (such as cod liver oil) to the diet of city children prevented the disease. Other oily substances, derived from plants, also worked, particularly if they were first irradiated with ultraviolet light. No one then knew what the irradiation was doing, and some pretty far-fetched theories were developed. Nevertheless it is easy to see how the substance concerned—called vitamin D, but not chemically identified until many years later—was classified as a vitamin. It was to rickets what thiamine was to beriberi, and what vitamin C was to scurvy. Where the early nutritionists went wrong will become clear when we tell the real story.

Vitamin D is produced by ultraviolet light from the sun acting on a compound derived from the cholesterol molecule. This reaction occurs in the middle layers of the skin of humans. Ultraviolet energy from sunlight is absorbed by the molecule and a chemical change occurs, resulting in vitamin D. The reaction is like what occurs when light acts on the silver grains of photographic film. The cholesterol-like compound is transformed into vitamin D, which then passes into blood vessels in the skin and is carried away to the rest of the body.

Other animals manufacture vitamin D out on the surfaces of their fur or feathers. Since the ultraviolet energy can't penetrate to their skin and there is no blood flow into the fur or feathers, these animals take in vitamin D through preening or grooming. The oil on fur or feathers contains vitamin D manufactured by exposure to the sunlight, and it is swallowed, absorbed through the intestine, and distributed in the body through the bloodstream.

Thus, the natural way for all animals to get vitamin D is through exposure to sunlight. Roughly fifteen minutes a day to hands, face, arms, and legs is probably sufficient to meet the needs of most humans. Much longer isn't beneficial because by the end of that time, the vitamin D produced piles up in the skin faster than the blood can carry it away, and when that happens the reaction stops. No more vitamin D is made until the backlog is cleared out of the skin, a process that can take hours.

Vitamin D, being a fatty molecule, dissolves readily in body fat, so it can be stored up in the summer for other times when we're less likely to get adequate solar exposure. Whether most of us make enough each summer to last all year is another matter. Clearly some of us—perhaps many of us—don't. But it is at least theoretically possible to do so.

Vitamin D, as made in the skin, is not yet biologically active. It is rapidly converted in the liver to a closely related compound called calcidiol, the principal storage form of the vitamin. Calcidiol is a very weak hormone, able to do very little to prevent rickets. But as the calcidiol molecules circulate in the bloodstream, some of them are further modified by the kidney into yet another compound, called calcitriol. This conversion is controlled by the amount of parathyroid hormone (PTH) circulating in the bloodstream. When PTH levels are high, we make a lot of calcitriol; when they are low, we make little or none. We encountered this part of the calcium regulatory system earlier. You'll recall that calcitriol is the signal to increase the efficiency of absorption of dietary calcium. While calcium can be absorbed without vitamin D, such absorption isn't very efficient. To increase absorption efficiency, calcitriol, derived from vitamin D, is needed. This hormone causes the cells lining the small intestine to make a special transport protein that binds calcium and shuttles it through the intestinal lining to the bloodstream. This active transport greatly increases the percentage of the calcium in food that can be successfully absorbed.

There are several other members of the vitamin D family of compounds in addition to calcitriol. They are also produced in the kidney, and they are chemically like calcitriol in a general way. No one knows for certain what their specific actions may be, and there is a lot of controversy about them, some scientists claiming that they are totally inactive and without biological significance. That seems doubtful. It would be very wasteful, in an evolutionary sense, to have all the cellular machinery to make these compounds if there were no use for them. It seems likely that compounds related to vitamin D are important to the function of several kinds of the bone cells—possibly to the damage-monitoring function of the osteocytes, and possibly also for the efficient functioning of the osteoblasts as they lay down new bone.

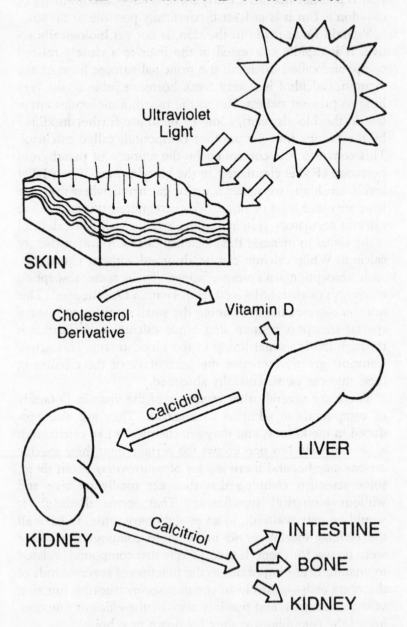

THE VITAMIN D PATHWAY

Ultraviolet
Light

SKIN

Cholesterol
Derivative

Vitamin D

Calcidiol

LIVER

KIDNEY

Calcitriol

INTESTINE

BONE

KIDNEY

As we noted earlier, a person might not need to make calcitriol if she were ingesting a very high-calcium diet, simply because she could absorb enough calcium to meet her needs. But it seems that not all the problems associated with a lack of vitamin D can be prevented by calcium alone. There are probably other vitamin D effects that are important to bone health. We have much more to learn about the vitamin D family of calcium-controlling hormones.

Now, back to where we started. You may have wondered why rickets was so common among children in northern and central European cities in the last century. The answer is air pollution. While our concern about air quality is quite a new phenomenon, the problem is old. A pall of smoke hung over much of Europe a hundred years ago, and it was made worse both by urban crowding and by the Industrial Revolution. The smoke was produced by inefficient burning of soft coal in factories, and by the burning of rubbish in hundreds of thousands of fireplaces and stoves used for cooking and heating. Smoke in the air blocked out most of the sun's rays for most of the year. In addition, child labor kept many city children indoors during the daytime. Finally, much of Europe is fairly far north of the equator, and is often rainy and cloudy. These factors together severely limited the amount of sun exposure that children received. They could not make enough vitamin D.

Are there health problems associated with inadequate vitamin D today? Probably not for most young people. We have cleaned up the air to a considerable extent. Young people are outdoors a great deal of the time, and they expose a lot of skin. We no longer tolerate child labor. In the United States, we are farther south than most of Europe, and hence the sun's rays do not have to go through quite so much atmosphere to reach the surface of the earth. Except possibly for chronically cloudy northern regions (such as along the eastern Great Lakes or in the Pacific Northwest), inadequate sunlight per se is not a significant factor in most of the United States.

But ultraviolet light from the sun does not go through glass, and so we have to go outdoors to benefit from it. It may be that, in the United States today, it is adults who are at risk for problems associated with vitamin D deficiency. Today many of us are indoors nearly all of the time. We enjoy fresh air and wide open spaces from inside our cars. Once we might have walked to work, or at least walked to the streetcar or bus stop—and thereby received some sunshine nearly every day. Now, often as not, we leave our homes to drive to work and spend all day in an office or factory. "Outdoor" athletic events increasingly take place indoors, in climate-controlled domes. Our sporadic play or exercise may be outdoors, but often it is not. Even going for a walk is becoming an indoor activity, in the phenomenon of "mall-walking." Sunscreens, advocated as protection against sunburn and skin cancer, unfortunately block the UV rays that make vitamin D. But you don't have to choose between skin cancer and vitamin D deficiency. A few minutes a day of skin exposure, particularly of different body parts, will not give you skin cancer.

The media and women's magazines have recently devoted a good deal of attention to the relationship between solar exposure and skin cancer. This is in response to the warnings of dermatologists about the danger of tanning. The dermatologists are right, but only to a point. Too much sun can be harmful, but no sun at all is harmful also. Rickets was a serious health problem among Northern European children only a few decades ago. And bone disease due to vitamin D deficiency is common even today among women in Muslim and Hindu societies that require seclusion and veiling. Yet an article in a recent issue of a women's magazine claimed that one should not even walk the dog around the block without protection by a sunscreen. It implied that *any* solar exposure is both undesirable, because it is responsible for aging of the skin, and dangerous, because it causes skin cancer. Such tunnel-visioned advice completely ignores the whole vitamin D issue, the very basic fact that some sun exposure is both natural for human beings and essential for health throughout life.

The risk of vitamin D deficiency due to inadequate exposure to sunlight is very high in the elderly, particularly those who are in institutions or homebound. We now know, from bone biopsies done in such individuals at the time of surgery for the repair of their various fractures, that they often have an adult version of rickets. This problem almost certainly contributes importantly to their greater bone fragility. A lack of vitamin D seems tragic because it is so easily preventable, either by assuring regular exposure to sunlight, or by taking a multiple-vitamin supplement that provides the daily requirement of vitamin D.

CALCIUM
AS A NUTRIENT

9

Calcium in Foods
and Beverages

Calcium is widely available in the food chain, and most animals, even those which eat only grasses and foliage, easily get all the calcium they need. But modern, civilized humans have developed dietary habits based on limited caloric intake —to match limited caloric expenditure—and relatively calcium-poor foods. Dairy products are the only major calcium-rich food source in the modern North American diet. But leafy green vegetables, shellfish, small bony fish, and certain nuts are also good sources of calcium.

Because calcium is necessary for life, all plants and animals contain some of it. Thus there is some calcium in all foods. And if drinking water is hard, as it is in many parts of the United States, we get calcium whenever we drink water— either directly or in beverages such as coffee or tea made from drinking water. (Of course, in softened water the calcium has been removed.) In many foods the amount of calcium is very small, particularly compared with the number of calories or other nutrients they contain; nevertheless, almost all natural foods contain some calcium, and if we ate enough of a broad variety of foods, we would likely get a balance of all nutrients, including calcium. (After all, dairy cows get enough calcium not only to make and maintain huge skeletons, but to produce every year 15,000 pounds of milk per cow, containing 9,000 grams of calcium!)

EXERCISE AND DIET

Think about a person who does hard physical work all day, particularly in the hot sun with a lot of sweating—as much of the human race has done for most of history—drinks a lot of water to slake a big thirst, and eats a lot of food to fuel the big energy expenditure. That person will probably get enough calcium, almost regardless of what is eaten, and without selecting calcium-rich foods. But how many of us live that way? Surely most of us don't.

Labor-saving devices have allowed most of us to cut our physical work down to almost nothing. Food intake has been cut drastically to match (or we would all be as obese as a circus fat lady). And when we get thirsty after cutting the grass or playing tennis, we don't drink tap water anymore, we drink a canned soft drink made from softened water.

The physical work of running a household—a large part of the daily caloric expenditure for many of us—is far less than it was just a few years ago. Compare washday in our grandparents' or great-grandparents' time and today: no carrying water, no washboards, no scrubbing, no hand wringing of clothes and hanging out on the line. In the kitchen are automatic dishwashers, electric can openers, even food processors. The machines we now take for granted are wonderfully useful and convenient, and it may be that people nowadays accomplish a good deal more each day than they could in the "good old days." But these conveniences have caused a profound reduction in physical work and caloric expenditure. It is hardly surprising that they have indirectly influenced nutrition.

As far as the calcium story is concerned, life-style changes have reduced both our total energy need and the work that stimulates the building of strong bones. Because we have reduced our food intake to match our energy output, we get much less of many critical nutrients than did our grandparents and great-grandparents. In recent years we have recognized that a typical woman in her reproductive years no longer gets enough iron from a typical diet to compensate for her monthly menstrual losses. We are just now beginning to realize that today's typical diet doesn't meet calcium needs, either.

There has been another life-style change for First World citizens that has affected our calcium intake—affluence. We may not feel affluent, but our foods are the foods of affluence. Only members of an affluent society can afford a high-protein diet. Meat is a relatively calcium-poor food, and per-person meat consumption has increased throughout this century in North America and Europe, both in total and as a fraction of total calories. Fats, too, are relatively expensive, and almost all fats are calcium-free. Thus, we fill up our limited caloric intakes with the foods of affluence—and unwittingly, but inevitably, cut down on calcium-rich foods.

We are not really interested in arguing against any of the changes that have taken place. But we do want to call attention to what has happened, as a basis for deep concern about getting enough dietary calcium. We want to explain why we need to be more concerned nowadays about calcium intake than would have been appropriate in our grandparents' time. It is important to see these life-style changes as the explanation for why, on a planet in which calcium is abundant virtually everywhere, human beings are confronted with the prospect—indeed, the likelihood—of a calcium-deficient diet.

THE CALCIUM CONTENT OF COMMON FOODS

For the first time in human history it is important to know which foods are good sources of calcium, to select foods that will meet our total nutrient needs. While we're watching calories, we have to make certain we don't eliminate foods that contain vital substances like calcium. The tables at the end of the chapter list the calcium content of many foods. All values are derived from USDA food tables or from analyses done in our own laboratory. The first table shows the calcium in typical servings of common foods. It doesn't show the foods by weight, as many food tables do, because customary servings of different foods often have quite different weights. The second table shows the calcium value per 100 calories, so you can see which foods give the most calcium value for their calories.

Sometimes we have provided ranges, but all of the figures should be considered approximate, for the nutrient content of all foods varies somewhat from place to place and season to season. The content of even some foods one might consider uniform, such as milk, will vary because different states have different milk standards.

- Among ordinary foods that are easily available to most of us, the most calcium-rich foods are dairy products. Single servings of Swiss cheese, low-fat yogurt, or low-fat milk, for instance, provide 272–452 milligrams of calcium. As we shall see in the next chapter, that is from one third to more than one half the adult recommended dietary allowance—and in just a single serving!

- There is an extremely broad range of calcium content in vegetables—from sweet corn, which is virtually calcium-free as we eat it in North America, to the dark green leafy vegetables (collard greens, dandelion, kale, lamb's-quarters, mustard, spinach, bok choy, and turnip greens), which range from spinach at 83 milligrams per serving to lamb's-quarters at 325 milligrams (more calcium per serving than a glass of whole milk).

- Meat and poultry are low in calcium. Seafood is somewhat higher, but varies a good bit among types. Shellfish, such as oysters and clams, are moderately good sources of calcium. All small fish eaten whole (such as sardines) are very rich in calcium. That's because we eat the bones, and bone is the richest source of calcium in the food chain. A single teaspoon of ground bone contains about 1,000 milligrams of calcium.

That raises an important point. We said that meat and poultry are low in calcium, and they are, if we analyze only the meat portion. But, as many experienced dietitians will attest, some people eat more than the meat. Some like to chew the tips of fried chicken wings, or the ends of the thigh or wing bones. In nutrition studies, this sort of behavior is usually not reported or analyzed, maybe because it is considered unrefined. But people in other cultures often nibble on bones. Perhaps bone chewing is not for everyone, but it is a good nutritional practice!

Bone isn't the only example of a food portion usually discarded but rich in calcium. Shrimp have a lot more calcium in their shells than in the meat. Fried shrimp generally contain the tips of the tail shells. Some people eat them; they like the crispy texture. Few dietitians ask about such a practice or record it. But a dozen tails contain about 500 milligrams of calcium. Primitive people, less fastidious than we, would have gotten a lot of calcium in what they consumed. The calcium content of canned salmon resides overwhelmingly in the bones it contains. If we remove the bones—perhaps as a gesture toward elegance—all of the calcium advantage of salmon is lost.

• Most cereal products are relatively poor sources of calcium, but several are now being enriched, either by adding calcium to the wheat flour used in baking, or by fortifying prepared breakfast foods. For instance, both Pillsbury and General Mills all-purpose white flour now have added calcium, and Pet Foods is now test marketing a breakfast cereal (Dairy Crisp) that is quite high in calcium. The widespread interest in calcium since 1982 makes it virtually certain that more and more companies will want to give their products a competitive advantage by fortifying with calcium. So check the labels.

- Most fruits (and hence fruit juices) are low in calcium. Oranges, orange juice, and papayas are the only exceptions among fruits generally available in North America. Some dried fruits, such as figs, raisins, and prunes are somewhat richer, mostly because they are concentrated, and so we eat more of them in one serving. Tropical fruits (amaranth, cherimoya, Indian fig, roselle, sapotes, and tamarinds) tend to be higher in calcium—some of them substantially so—but because they are not widely available in North America, we have not listed them.

- Nuts vary widely. Almonds, hazelnuts (filberts), and brazil nuts are the best calcium sources among those nuts generally available in North America. Interestingly, some natural sweeteners turn out to be relatively rich in calcium, particularly maple syrup and molasses. In the latter case, the early extraction—light molasses—contains less calcium than do the later extractions.

The last portion of the tables at the end of this chapter gives some idea of the cost in calories of the calcium we need. In this table, the calcium sources rearrange themselves. The dark green leafy vegetables are now clearly out front. These are low-calorie sources, so they are excellent calcium bargains. Four are so high in calcium that it would be possible to get all the calcium a mature adult needs each day at a cost of 100 calories or less. Ten would provide for daily calcium need at a cost under 200 calories.

Low-fat dairy products are second in line. All the calcium an adult needs costs only 200–400 calories for most of the dairy products listed. Second place does not, of course, mean that dairy products are not as good nutritionally as leafy vegetables. Quite the contrary. Dairy products are far richer in protein than most vegetables. But protein in food contributes energy—calories, that is—as well as the building blocks of tissues, so inevitably the calcium-per-calorie figure will be lower than one would find in protein-poor foods, such as the leafy vegetables.

After that, the best calcium-to-calorie ratio is found in oysters, shellfish, and bone-containing canned fish. Sardines, you will note, drop below canned salmon in Table II (whereas they are ahead in Table I), but only because of the calorie-rich oil that sardines are usually packed in.

We could not leave these tables without another note about affluence. In the past the dark green leafy vegetables were often the food of poor people and slaves, both because they couldn't afford to throw any part of a food item away, and because the greens were sometimes left over after the servants had prepared food for others. Today, a similar irony appears in the various types of frozen broccoli. Chopped broccoli contains leaves and stems, whereas packaged whole broccoli stalks contain no leaves at all. The chopped is, therefore, substantially cheaper. But most of the calcium is in the leaves. So those who can choose a "better" type of broccoli get less calcium.

FOOD FADS

Many people wonder about the effects of processing on nutritional value. In most cases this concern has been caused by promoters of nutrition quackery who, in order to push their so-called "natural" products or methods, claim that ordinary foods have been degraded by modern methods of agriculture, harvesting, and processing. This is simply not true, certainly not true for calcium. There is absolutely nothing to the claim that cooking or pasteurization or any other process reduces the nutritive value of calcium in a food. Extensive tests of absorption have left no doubt whatsoever that calcium is just as available from say, cooked vegetables as from raw (there are good reasons to prefer raw vegetables, but calcium availability is not one of them). We are also frequently asked, "Doesn't pasteurizing milk make the calcium less available?" The answer is *no!* We have tested many different dairy products in our laboratories at Creighton, using the best methods science has to offer. We have found that calcium is just about as available from one dairy product as another. There is no reason to believe that pasteurization makes any difference in the absorption and retention of dairy product calcium.

People ask also about mixing different foods. Does this alter calcium availability? The answers are not all in. Here is the best we can tell you right now. Spinach contains a substance called oxalic acid that binds with calcium and interferes with its absorption. But spinach contains enough calcium to use up all the oxalic acid. So the worst that can happen is that the spinach calcium will not be absorbable. So far as we know, a glass of milk drunk at the same meal with a serving of spinach will provide as much calcium as the same milk drunk at any other time.

Other food substances, such as phytic acid, found in certain whole-grain cereals, are also said to bind calcium, but their practical effect on calcium availability from other foods is probably slight. One of the reasons for this statement is that foods containing a calcium binder will bind calcium contained in the digestive juices if there isn't much calcium in the foods eaten at the same meal. The net effect on our calcium economies is about the same either way. Does that mean that foods containing calcium binders should be avoided? No. They contain many other important nutrients. Their calcium binding is one example of how all nutrients interact.

There are many strange diets popular today, some new, some old, many potentially dangerous. There is the notion that a diet of very limited variety might be good. There is the notion that certain foods should never be eaten at the same meal with other foods, such as the idea—espoused in the bestseller *Fit for Life*—that carbohydrate and protein foods are incompatible. There is the notion that adults were never meant to consume milk, and therefore that the "natural" requirement for calcium must be very low. This is outright quackery.

In discussing fads it is useful to look even further to examine underlying values. We might think, for example, about style, fashion, and values as they are reflected in the advertising for women's clothing. Indeed, if fashion models reflect the ideals or values of the culture, then our ideal woman looks like someone who has been ill for a long time with a wasting disease. We need to think about whether it is more feminine and appropriate to be emaciated or strong, to be helpless or capable. One would hope that few women today would buy weakness and helplessness as necessary or appropriate expressions of their femininity.

The notion that thinness is somehow healthy—let alone required for acceptance by others—is both peculiar and dangerous. Recall the saying "You can't be too thin or too rich." We laugh, but do we really disagree? Still it is quite possible to be too thin. A style of eating and living that only wealth can buy is often associated with both calcium deficiency and physical inactivity. Also, over a period of years it means too little load on the skeletal structure and consequent skeletal deterioration.

The fad of thinness has another, more directly harmful effect. Anorexia/bulimia is an enormous problem. These are serious eating disorders in young women who become mistaken about their own body images (and always seem fat to themselves), or who get caught in a cycle of binge-and-purge, overeating, and self-induced vomiting. The long-term implications of these disorders for the physical and psychological health of these women are frightening. Psychiatrists are convinced that the fad of thinness, communicated through advertisements and the media, is responsible for the epidemic of these disorders.

THE CALCIUM CONTENT OF COMMON FOODS

	Serving Size	*Calcium (mg)* per serving
CHEESES		
Swiss	1 oz	272
Monterey Jack	1 oz	212
Colby	1 oz	194
Cheddar	1 oz	204
American	1 oz	174
Roquefort	1 oz	188
Brie	1 oz	52
Ricotta, part skim	1/2 cup	337
Parmesan	1 tbsp	69
Cottage	1/2 cup	68
YOGURTS		
Plain, low-fat or skim	1 cup	415–452
Fruit-flavored, low fat	1 cup	314
MILKS		
Skim	1 cup	302–316
Low-fat	1 cup	297–313
Whole	1 cup	288
Chocolate	1 cup	280–290
Nonfat dry	2 oz	292
ICE CREAM	1 cup	150–230
VEGETABLES		
Asparagus	1/2 cup	15
Avocado	1 med	19
Bean sprouts	2 oz	30
Beans, kidney	1/2 cup	47
Beans, lima	1/2 cup	37
Beans, string (green)	1 cup	62
Beans, white	1/2 cup	50
Beet greens	2 oz	68
Beets	1/2 cup	12

	Serving Size	Calcium (mg) per serving
Bok choy (Chinese Cabbage)	1 cup	160
Broccoli	3-1/2 oz (1 lg stalk)	88
Brussels sprouts	3-1/2 oz (6–8 med)	32
Cabbage	1 cup	49
Carrots	3 oz (1 large)	36
Cauliflower	3-1/2 oz	42
Celery	1 stalk	20
Collard greens	1/2 cup	152
Corn	1/2 cup	5
Cucumbers with skin	1/2 med	13
Dandelion Greens	3-1/2 oz	187
Dulse (seaweed)	1 oz	85
Kale	3-1/2 oz	134
Kelp (seaweed)	1 oz	325
Kohlrabi	1/2 cup	25
Lamb's-quarters	3-1/2 oz	309
Lettuce, iceberg	3-1/2 oz	20
Mustard greens	1/2 cup	138
Okra	3-1/2 oz (8-9 pods)	92
Onions, chopped	1 tbsp	3
Parsnips	1/2 cup	45
Peas, green	1/2 cup	17
Peas, snow (pea pods)	1/2 cup	49
Pepper, sweet (bell)	1 large	9
Potatoes, sweet	1/2 cup	30
Potatoes, whole, with skin	1 med	7
Rice	1/2 cup	12
Rutabaga	1/2 cup	59
Scallions	4 med	32
Spinach	1/2 cup	83
Tofu	1 oz	37
Tomatoes	1 small	13
Turnip greens	1/2 cup	138
Watercress	1 oz	56
Zucchini	1/2 cup	17

	Serving Size	Calcium (mg) per serving
MEATS, POULTRY, EGGS, FISH, AND SEAFOOD		
Eggs	1	27
Poultry	3-1/2 oz	15–20
Beef, pork, lamb, veal (lean only)	3-1/2 oz	6–12
Liver, calves'	3-1/2 oz	13
Shrimp	3-1/2 oz	63
Clams	3-1/2 oz	96
Oysters	3-1/2 oz (5–8 med)	94
Whitefish	3-1/2 oz	20–60
Sardines, canned, with bones	3-1/2 oz	354
Salmon, canned, with bones	1/2 cup	325
SYRUPS		
Molasses, light	1 tbsp	33
Molasses, medium	1 tbsp	58
Molasses, blackstrap	1 tbsp	116
Maple syrup	1 tbsp	33
CEREAL PRODUCTS		
Enriched white or wheat bread	2 slices	60
English muffin	1	92
Noodles	1 cup	14
Spaghetti	1 cup	16
NUTS		
Almonds	1/2 oz	38
Brazil nuts	1/2 oz	28
Cashews	1/2 oz	6
Hazelnuts (filberts)	1/2 oz	38
Peanuts	1/2 oz	9
Pecans	1/2 oz	11
Pistachios	1/2 oz	22

	Serving Size	Calcium (mg) per serving
Walnuts, English	1/2 oz	12
Peanut butter	1 oz	22
FRUITS		
Apples	1 med	10
Bananas	1 med	7
Blueberries	1 cup	9
Cantaloupe	1 cup	17
Cherries	2 oz	9
Grapes	1 cup	13
Oranges	1 med	56
Papayas	1 cup	50
Peaches	1 med	5
Pears	1 med	19
Plums	1 large	3
Raspberries	1 cup	27
Strawberries	1 cup	21

CALCIUM-TO-CALORIE RATIOS

	Calcium (mg) per 100 calories
CHEESES	
Swiss	254
Monterey Jack	200
Colby	173
Cheddar	179
American	164
Roquefort	179
Brie	55
Ricotta, part skim	197
Parmesan	303
Cottage	58

	Calcium (mg) *per* *100 calories*
YOGURTS	
Plain, low-fat or skim	288
Fruit-flavored, low-fat	140
ICE CREAM	40–75
MILKS	
Whole	192
2%	245
Skim	351
Non-fat, dry	346
SYRUPS	
Molasses, light	66
Molasses, medium	125
Molasses, blackstrap	272
Maple syrup	41
VEGETABLES	
Beans (string), green	200
Beet greens	496
Bok choy (Chinese cabbage)	1,600
Broccoli	322
Cabbage	204
Collard greens	507
Corn	6
Dandelion greens	416
Kale	471
Kohlrabi	137
Lamb's-quarters	806
Lettuce, iceberg	154
Mustard greens	590
Okra	317
Onions	71
Peas, green	31
Potatoes, sweet	28

Calcium (mg)
per
100 calories

Potatoes, whole, with skin	9
Rutabaga	169
Scallions	89
Spinach	358
Tofu	178
Tomatoes	59
Turnip greens	920
Watercress	795

MEATS, POULTRY, EGGS, FISH, SEAFOOD

Eggs	35
Poultry	6–15*
Beef, pork, lamb, veal (lean only)	2–5*
Liver, calves'	5
Shrimp	69
Clams	86
Oysters	142
Sardines, canned, with bones	144
Salmon, canned with bones	151

NUTS

Almonds	42
Brazil nuts	29
Cashews	7
Hazelnuts (filberts)	39
Peanuts	12
Pecans	11
Pistachios	22
Walnuts, English	13
Peanut butter	13

	Calcium (mg) per 100 calories
FRUITS	
Apples	12
Bananas	6
Blueberries	11
Cantaloupe	33
Cherries	20
Grapes	25
Oranges	86
Papayas	62
Peaches	14
Pears	19
Plums	6
Raspberries	44
Strawberries	47

* Values will be substantially lower than shown if fat is included in serving.

10
Calcium Requirements and Allowances

Each of us has an individual requirement for calcium that is different from other people's and different at different times of our lives. In general, though, people need a lot of calcium during growth and pregnancy, and while nursing. Recently we have learned that older adults also have high calcium requirements, partly because they don't use dietary calcium efficiently. Government-sponsored Recommended Dietary Allowances (RDAs) do not yet acknowledge that skeletal growth extends to the middle years or that women past the menopause need more calcium.

Knowing how much calcium a food contains is only the first step. Naturally you also have to know how much you need. To answer that question, as well as to help you understand claims made by food processors and to read their labels intelligently, you need to understand two important nutritional concepts, requirement and allowance. Doing this will also help you understand why you continue to need calcium throughout life, and why the level of your need changes at different periods during life.

WHAT IS A "REQUIREMENT"?

All nutrients have a requirement, the amount a person must take in every day to maintain health—which generally, for adults, means to offset the amount of the nutrient spent, lost, or utilized each day. For most nutrients, we now know what these values are, at least in general. For some, we don't yet know how much is required, only that we do require *some.*

Calories in food are a familiar illustration of a dietary requirement. Calories are an expression of the energy content of food. When we think of energy for home heating or cooling, we use such units as BTUs (for British Thermal Units), but the concepts are exactly the same. In one case the fuel provides the energy for the work of our bodies, and in the other the energy for heating or cooling our homes.

From their association with weight control, one might think calories were a bad thing. But the fact is, we need them, for they power our muscles and all other tissue activities as well, and they maintain our body temperature, just as other fuels run engines and heat buildings. Clearly we *require* calories, just as engines require fuel. If we don't take in as much as we use each day—that is, if we take in less than we require —then we start to burn our own tissues for fuel. When that can no longer be done, people starve to death.

We need many, many nutrients. There are requirements for organic compounds such as protein, essential fatty acids, and vitamins; for bulk minerals such as calcium, phosphorus, sodium, potassium, and magnesium; and even for trace elements, such as cobalt, iron, manganese, zinc, copper, and many others. For the organic compounds, the requirement comes about because some of the nutrient is used up every day in the process of doing its job, and for the minerals, because some is lost every day (principally through excretion). In both cases, the requirement reflects our need to replace what is used or lost.

Requirements vary from person to person, sometimes to a considerable extent. This should not be surprising. It makes sense that a person doing hard physical work requires more energy from food—more calories—than does a sedentary person. Burning a lot of energy through hard physical work uses up some other nutrients, too. Thus persons deprived of vitamin C will get scurvy sooner if they are working hard than if they are inactive. Their stores of vitamin C are used up more quickly. But even for similar levels of work, requirements vary widely from person to person. Some people require more sleep than others. Some require more quiet than others. Some seem to be able to stand more discomfort than others. In just the same way, some require more of a certain nutrient than do other people. Some of the difference is due to differences in body size, some to physical activity, some to the amounts of other foods we take in, some to life-style factors such as smoking and coffee drinking, some to sickness or medications. But even after we have allowed for all these, there still are large differences due to genetic factors.

If we could determine the requirement for any single nutrient for every person—or at least for a random sample—the results could be expressed like the following diagram. While

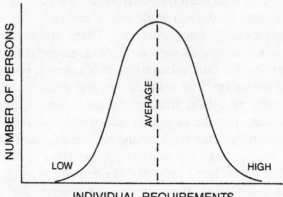

a few people would have a high requirement, and a few would have a low requirement, most would be near a central value. That central value is the average requirement.

We also might move along the scale of individual requirement values from lowest to highest, asking ourselves at each step, "How many persons have requirements less than or equal to this level?" The answers would produce another diagram, somewhat like the one on p. 71, which shows, for each requirement value, the proportion of the population with an actual requirement equal to or less than that value. Notice that the curve rises slowly at first, because not very many people have low requirements. As we move toward the middle of the range, where most of the people are located, even a small change in the requirement produces a large change in the number of people who fall below it. And then, finally, as we get toward the high end of the requirement range, the curve rises much more slowly once again, simply because not very many people are left who have very high requirements.

WHAT IS AN "ALLOWANCE"?

The diagram on p. 71 contains information that is important in understanding the notion of an allowance. Whereas a requirement describes the need of an individual person, an allowance is a public policy statement, used to guide diet therapy and certain government food programs. It is a value equivalent to about the 95th percentile of all requirements for that nutrient (point A in the diagram). That is, 95 percent of all individuals in a population have requirements equal to or less than (and mostly less than) the allowance value.

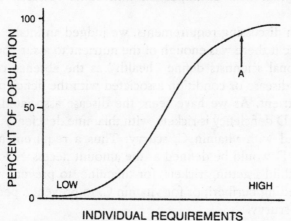

CUMULATIVE DISTRIBUTION OF NUTRIENT REQUIREMENTS

An allowance is a public policy statement because it is used to guide various public actions. Thus, school lunch programs and food stamp programs attempt to assure an intake (or at least buying power sufficient to obtain an intake) equal to or exceeding the actual requirement for 95 percent of all persons. In other words, they provide more than most people need, but will assure that most persons will get at least as much as they need. Nevertheless, about 5 percent of the people, one in 20, will need still more.

Wouldn't the average requirement be a better basis for public policy decisions? No. If we saw to it that everyone got the average requirement, then about half the population would not be getting as much as they require. To assure adequate nutrition for only half the population would not be good public policy. So the figure for an allowance must be set high enough to get above the actual requirement for the great majority of the population.

Allowances are generally expressed as Recommended Dietary Allowances (RDAs), and most of the First World nations have developed allowances for most nutrients. In some cases the values are firmly based; in others they are largely guesswork, but still better than no numbers at all. (There is still a great deal of important nutritional research to be done.)

When discussing requirements, we judged an intake to be adequate if there was enough of the nutrient to assure health. Nutritional scientists define "health" as the absence of the specific disease or condition associated with the deficiency of that nutrient. As we have seen, the disease associated with vitamin D deficiency is rickets, with thiamine deficiency, beriberi, and with vitamin C, scurvy. Thus a requirement for vitamin D would be defined as the amount necessary to prevent a child's getting rickets; for thiamine, to prevent a person's getting beriberi; or for vitamin C, to prevent a person's getting scurvy.

The problem with this approach is that it is circular. There could be another condition caused by a milder deficiency— not enough to produce the criterion disease—and yet it might be so widespread that we failed to recognize it as a treatable problem. We might have considered it, for example, as just a part of normal aging. This is the basis for a controversy that surrounds many nutrients today. For example, some scientists, such as Linus Pauling, claim we need a great deal more vitamin C than the figure enshrined as the RDA. Others claim that we need more vitamin A. And so forth.

The evidence in most such cases is very weak, or at least indirect, and health policymakers have decided that they need *strong* evidence before formulating policy applicable to a whole nation. Thus, in general, the committees tend to be conservative. Probably most of the claims for higher requirements will prove to have been groundless, and the conservative posture of the scientific boards and panels responsible for setting public policy will have served us well. Nevertheless, the possibility remains that the absence of a single, specific disease is not the best criterion for judging the adequacy of intake of some nutrients, including, as we will see, calcium and vitamin D.

One might think that RDAs would be the same, or nearly the same, in all countries. After all, science is science. But nutritional science is less than exact, and scientists disagree over its findings. A brief glimpse of the calcium RDAs for mature adults shows a surprising amount of variation among nations:

United States	800 mg
Canada	700–800 mg
United Kingdom	500 mg
Japan	600 mg
World Health Organization	400–500 mg

Some of this variability is related to differences in body size. Thus, the Japanese and U.S. values are closer than they seem, when expressed per unit body weight of the typical citizen. However, there still is a twofold difference between the low World Health Organization figure (400 milligrams) and the high U.S. figure (800 milligrams). This discrepancy reflects politics, disagreements among scientists, and actual differences in requirements (for example, people in the Third World get less protein, so need less calcium).

We will explore some of the controversy surrounding the RDA for calcium later. For the moment, though, you should know that there has been a shift in the scientific consensus recently, toward higher numbers, especially for women ten years before and after menopause. Here are some recent RDAs for women aged forty to sixty:

Official U.S. RDA (1980)	800 mg
U.S. Committee on RDAs 1985— recommendation not yet adopted	1,000 mg
National Institutes of Health (NIH) Consensus Panel on Osteoporosis (1984)	
—for estrogen-replete women	1,000 mg
—for estrogen-deprived women	1,500 mg
Food & Nutrition Board of the Netherlands (1985)	1,000 mg

These last four numbers, which are higher than any of the current national RDAs, reflect a growing realization that women near and after menopause may need more calcium than when they were younger, and that the loss of estrogen at menopause further increases calcium need.

ALLOWANCES FOR THE TIMES OF OUR LIVES.

The change in RDA for middle-aged women reflects the generally recognized fact that requirements for many nutrients are different at different times of our lives. Growth, pregnancy, and lactation are other special times, with special needs, as are the years from forty to sixty.

The official RDA values for calcium, last published by the Committee on Dietary Allowances of the National Research Council in 1980, are as follows:

Children aged 2–12	800 mg
Adolescents aged 12–19	1,200 mg
Adults aged 19 and over	800 mg
Pregnant women	1,200 mg
Lactating women	1,200 mg

The RDA for a two-year-old is set as high as that for an adult, who is likely to weigh 6 to 10 times as much. The growing child needs to build bones, and so needs a lot of calcium. This need increases during adolescence—the time of greatest bone building—and so the allowance rises to 1,200 milligrams. It has only recently been recognized that bone continues to increase in density and weight past adolescence, indeed throughout the twenties. Unfortunately this fact is not reflected in the drop of the RDA from 1,200 to 800 at age nineteen. It seems likely that the 1,200-milligram figure for adolescents ought to be extended to age thirty. Finally, the 1,200-milligram figure for pregnancy and lactation clearly reflect the need to build a baby's skeleton—both in the womb and at the breast.

In the 1980 edition of the Recommended Dietary Allowances, no distinction was made between adult men and women, and no special provision was made for the decline in efficiency of utilization of dietary calcium that occurs at menopause in women and in older persons of both sexes, and which increases the actual calcium requirement. It is likely that more countries will raise the RDA for middle-aged women, and possibly also for older persons of both sexes.

READING LABELS.

Many food labels contain nutrition information about a typical serving. Usually for each nutrient the label tells the "percent of U.S.R.D.A." What does this mean? Which one of the various RDA figures do such labels refer to? Actually, to none of them.

The RDAs we have been referring to (for calcium and other nutrients, varying for different ages and different physiological states) are a kind of gold standard for the country. They are produced every five or six years by the National Research Council of the National Academy of Sciences, a public but nongovernmental body funded by Congress to deal with many issues of public policy which depend upon the sciences. But the information on food packages comes from the Food and Drug Administration, a branch of the

Department of Health and Human Services of the federal government. The FDA has responsibility not only for drugs, but for certain aspects of food purity, safety, and labeling. Recognizing that it would be far too complicated to list several sets of numbers (to show, for example, that a serving of breakfast cereal provides 18 percent of what a child needs of a nutrient, but only 12 percent of what an adolescent needs), the FDA settled on an average of the various figures for different ages and physiological states. For calcium, that average figure is 1,000 milligrams per day. Thus, when a carton of milk is said to contain 30 percent of the U.S.R.D.A. for calcium, that means that it contains about 30 percent of 1,000 milligrams, or about 300 milligrams.

The so-called U.S.R.D.A.s for all nutrients are simply averages of the specific RDAs for the various ages and conditions.

11

How Other Foods Affect Your Body's Use of Calcium

Many other components of our diets modify our need for calcium. Protein and caffeine increase urinary losses of calcium. High-fiber diets speed food through the intestine faster, and hence reduce absorption of calcium. These and other factors raise our individual requirement for dietary calcium.

It is important to describe the interactions between calcium and other nutrients for two reasons. First, because you have heard a lot about them; some of that information is accurate, some not. But even the accurate information is hard to interpret if you don't understand how nutrients interact and what it all means. Second, nutrient interactions explain some of the differences in requirements between both individuals and populations. So this chapter helps prepare you for more detailed discussion of that topic in the next chapter.

Simply put, how much we need of a nutrient is determined in part by all the other things we eat. Calcium is no exception. These interactions simply reflect the fact that a requirement depends in part upon the rest of the diet.

Calcium Interactions

Nutrient	Effect	Why?
Fiber	Negative	Decreases intestinal absorption of calcium
Protein	Negative	Increases urinary loss of calcium
Caffeine	Negative	Increases both urinary and intestinal loss of calcium
Sodium	Negative	Increases urinary loss of calcium
Phosphorus	Neutral	Decreases urinary loss of calcium; increases intestinal loss of calcium
Certain sugars	Positive	Increase intestinal absorption of calcium

Interactions may be positive, neutral, or negative. Negative effects are not, in themselves, harmful, and certainly are not an indication that the nutrient responsible should be avoided.

Fiber

Fiber is a good example. The human organism, as it has evolved, seems to have been adapted to a high fiber content in the diet. Fiber provides bulk, holds water, and moves undigested food residue rapidly through the intestine. We have come to recognize in recent years that low-fiber diets lead to slow movement of food residues and allow intestinal bacteria more time to convert fecal materials into potentially cancer-causing chemicals. In this way, a low-fiber diet increases our risk of colon cancer, while a high-fiber diet affords some protection against it. Clearly, assuring sufficient fiber in our diets is good.

But if intestinal contents move through the gut more rapidly, there is less time for calcium to be absorbed. Also, the fiber molecules may themselves bind some of the calcium in our food and carry it out of the body. For both reasons a person on a high-fiber diet has a higher calcium requirement. However, within the range of fiber intakes likely to be encountered in most North American diets, the effect is relatively small, and the positive effects of fiber far outweigh this negative effect on calcium. Thus there is no reason whatsoever to be concerned about bone health while consuming a reasonably high-fiber intake, nor is there any reason to try to space the intake of calcium-rich foods so they won't mix with fiber-containing foods.

Protein

The ordinary wear and tear on tissues means that some of the building blocks of body proteins need to be replaced every day. That is why protein is an essential part of the diet, even for adults who are no longer growing. However, if we eat more protein than we need for this tissue replacement, the surplus is burned as fuel. The breakdown products of this excess protein increase the loss of calcium through the kidneys.

One of those breakdown products is sulfuric acid, which

draws some calcium out with it when it is eliminated by the kidney. So increased protein intake increases urine calcium loss. The chemical process is basically the same one that happens when sulfur-containing fossil fuels are burned in industry. It is the the acid rain problem writ small. Bones are depleted as calcium is lost through the kidneys, just as limestone buildings and statues (also made of calcium) are dissolved by acid rain.

Taking in more protein than we need increases calcium loss in the urine. As with fiber, it doesn't mean we shouldn't eat protein. But as protein intake goes up, our personal requirement for calcium goes up, too.

Can we put some tentative numbers to this? Experiments from three different laboratories indicate that doubling a person's protein intake leads to a 50 percent increase in urinary calcium loss. So the effect is far from negligible. Thus, if a 120-pound woman were to increase her protein intake from 44 to 88 grams per day (not an unusual intake in the United States), her urine calcium loss would increase by about 50–60 milligrams. If her calcium absorption efficiency were in the range of 25–30 percent (as it commonly is in middle-aged women), she would have to increase her calcium intake by about 200–300 milligrams (equivalent to nearly an extra glass of milk each day) to compensate for this additional protein-induced loss.

The relationship of calcium requirement to fiber and protein isn't a problem for most animals, simply because their natural diets usually contain an abundance of calcium. But it can be a problem for people living in the First World, because so many of us have calcium intakes at or below the borders of deficiency. And anything that increases the requirement for calcium aggravates the deficiency. But the problem can be prevented by increasing calcium intake to match protein intake. Or by not taking in a great deal more protein than we really need.

How much protein *do* we need? The RDA for a mature woman weighing 120 pounds is 44 grams a day. That's roughly the amount of protein in two Big Macs, or one half of a 12-inch pizza, or a double hamburger, or two pork chops. That's not very much protein. Most North Americans get a great deal more than that every day, and that excess aggravates the problem of our generally low calcium intake.

Caffeine

Caffeine increases the loss of calcium in the urine, possibly through digestive secretions, and probably through sweat as well, but this has not yet been sufficiently studied. However, the effect is generally quite small, and, at moderate caffeine intakes, is almost negligible. Thus the small additional loss of calcium caused by two to three cups of coffee a day can be more than offset by just a few tablespoons of milk (or any equivalent calcium-containing food). Caffeine becomes a calcium problem principally when it is consumed to great excess, e.g., 20 cups of coffee a day. Usually such heavy coffee drinkers don't drink much milk. (After all, one can consume only so much liquid in a day.) Also, heavy coffee drinkers often smoke, which itself aggravates the risk of developing osteoporosis). The combination of these three negative factors in the typical coffee addict compounds the harmful effects of each individual factor.

Sodium

The body absorbs sodium very well from the intestine, reflecting the evolutionary fact that sodium is a scarce mineral in the environment of land-living animals, and so absorption has had to be efficient. Now, of course, most of us can easily get a great deal more sodium than we need.

Sodium is probably not as bad for us as some people interested in hypertension would have us think (see Chapter 22). But we don't store extra sodium, and the body must eliminate it. This is done with remarkable efficiency through the kidneys. However, the elimination of sodium leads to increased elimination of calcium as well. In practical terms, the daily requirement for calcium is higher if we eat a lot of salty foods than it would be otherwise.

Phosphorus

There is a public and professional awareness of the interaction of phosphorus with calcium that is all out of proportion to its importance. Phosphorus *does* increase the calcium lost in the digestive juices, but it also *decreases* the loss of calcium through the kidneys. The two effects cancel one another.

Why all the concern? It may be related to nutritional research on rapidly growing young animals, infants, and children, for whom calcium and phosphorus are crucial for building bone and other tissues. To support their rapid growth, the body keeps the concentration of phosphorus high in the extracellular fluid. When the level of phosphorus in the extracellular fluid is high, too much phosphorus in the diet *can* upset the calcium economy. But high phosphorus levels in the extracellular fluid occur only in children—not in adults. Further, in adults growth is no longer a factor, and the balance of nutrients is no longer so critical as it is during infancy.

In any case, several studies have looked at the effect of phosphorus on bone and calcium. The FDA, for instance, convened a panel of scientists in 1981 to look at all aspects of phosphorus intake in the American diet. The agency was acting in response to the increase in phosphorus intake associated particularly with increased consumption of soft drinks. But, after reviewing the data on all sides of the issue, the panel concluded that it was, in essence, a nonproblem. The problem with soft drinks—if any—lies in the fact that they are being substituted for tap water and other calcium-containing beverages in the American diet, not that their phosphorus is itself harmful.

Sugars

It has been known for many years that lactose, or milk sugar, aids calcium absorption in certain laboratory animals. The data from human beings is much less clear, but it appears that having lactose, or possibly any simple sugar, in the intestine may have a slight beneficial effect on calcium absorption. Since most ordinary meals contain carbohydrates—which break down in the intestine to simple sugars—the net effect in adults is small and probably makes little practical difference.

However, people with intestinal abnormalities, such as those who have had surgery resulting in a shortening of the bowel, do show a definite benefit from consuming certain types of sugars or starches with calcium-containing foods. These substances help them absorb the calcium they need.

We mention this effect of sugars primarily for the sake of completeness, and because one comes upon this point in articles about nutrition in the popular press. Various authors, some representing themselves as nutritionists, have come upon isolated reports in the scientific literature and uncritically applied them to everyone. We do not believe that sugar is of much practical importance for calcium availability in most adults, and we want to stress that it is *not* something most of us need to worry about.

In fact, worrying about nutrition is probably the wrong approach altogether. While it is our thesis in this book that most of us would be better off consuming more calcium, there are relatively simple, straightforward ways to accomplish this. We believe that once habits have been changed, the whole matter ought to be put out of our minds. We frequently encounter questions about whether one should space calcium intake so that calcium-containing foods won't mix in the intestine with fiber-containing foods (as mentioned above), or with certain vegetables (such as spinach, which contain calcium-binding oxalate) and the like. This kind of concern seems to us to convert eating into a carefully regulated project in chemical engineering, requiring a great deal of careful attention. We think that approach takes all the fun out of eating. People who urge us to adopt such meticulous control have an odd perspective.

12

Why You May Need More Calcium Than Someone Else Does

Absorption of calcium from the diet is ordinarily inefficient. Mature adults absorb only 30–35 percent of the calcium from a typical diet. This fraction falls with age, and is commonly 25 percent or less after menopause. Once calcium is absorbed and incorporated into the skeleton, it is better conserved by some people than others. So some people need less in their diets. By contrast, others eliminate calcium easily—too easily, perhaps. So they need to consume more—in some cases a lot more.

There are as many reasons for calcium requirements to differ from person to person as there are people. Ultimately our capacity to get by on a certain level of any nutrient is determined in part by the same kind of genetic program that determines whether our eyes are blue or our hair curly. But in addition to this genetic diversity, there are environmental, dietary, and personal influences as well, as we have already seen. Three factors influence the individual requirement for calcium: obligatory loss; intestinal absorption efficiency; and responsiveness of bone to calcium-regulating hormones.

OBLIGATORY LOSS

Obligatory loss is the daily loss of calcium that cannot be avoided. Obligatory loss becomes important when the body has to adjust to scarce calcium. Then the amount lost every day determines how much must be absorbed to avoid tearing down bone for its calcium. What determines how large that loss is? Genetic differences, for one thing. But certain dietary factors—such as caffeine, protein, and sodium—are important also, because they increase the loss of calcium through the kidneys. That's why we discussed nutritional interactions in the last chapter.

We repeat here, as we did there, that caffeine, protein, and sodium are not harmful in themselves. But if the amount of calcium ingested or absorbed is very low, then any excess of sodium, protein, or caffeine—which increase obligatory loss —will aggravate the calcium deficiency. Probably the major differences in calcium requirement between individuals of different races and nations—apart from genetic influences— are due to the striking differences in protein, sodium, and caffeine intake. A typical white female in North America or the United Kingdom has an obligatory loss of about 180 milligrams of calcium per day. People in other countries may well have an average loss only half as great, perhaps even less. Clearly the level of minimum obligatory loss is an important determinant of calcium requirement.

INTESTINAL ABSORPTION EFFICIENCY

We absorb only about one third of the calcium we take in. (This inefficiency is an evolutionary adaptation to the overall abundance of calcium in foodstuffs, and, as we shall see in the next chapter, to the fact that a human being would consume a surplus of calcium under natural conditions.) Because many people in the First World do not have diets providing a surplus of calcium, the ability to increase absorption efficiency has become crucial.

When some people need more calcium, they just absorb more from what they are already eating. Many teens and young adults can make the best of even bad diets. But for others, particularly middle-aged and elderly women, the system seems sluggish. Absorption fails to rise sufficiently when intake is low or when minimum obligatory loss is high. As a result, bone is lost. No one knows what the exact reasons are. There may be a shortage of vitamin D, either because of inadequate exposure to the sun or because the kidneys are sluggish in their manufacture of calcitriol, the calcium-absorbing hormone made from vitamin D.

BONE RESPONSIVENESS

We noted earlier (Chapter 3) that parathyroid hormone (PTH) keeps the level of calcium in the extracellular fluid at optimal levels by (1) decreasing the loss of calcium in the urine, (2) increasing the absorption efficiency of calcium from the diet, and (3) increasing the release of calcium from bone through enhanced bone destruction.

The parathyroid glands produce PTH in response to changes in calcium levels in the extracellular fluid. But they have no way of telling whether the three remote target organs—kidney, intestine, and bone—are each contributing their fair share. The glands continue to pour out PTH, in larger and larger quantities if necessary, until calcium levels rise, regardless of how the job is accomplished. For example, in a person who is not eating or whose diet contains little calcium, the absorptive effect of PTH will contribute little or nothing to a higher calcium level. The parathyroid glands don't "know" this; they simply drive all three of the mechanisms harder. The ones that can respond do so; the ones that can't, don't. Clearly, having three independent mechanisms for maintaining extracellular calcium is insurance against a low calcium level.

But consider what would happen if one of these three targets of PTH were made either more resistant or more responsive to PTH action. Take bone responsiveness. If the bones are hyperresponsive to PTH, then they will contribute more than their fair share to keeping the extracellular fluid calcium levels up. The kidneys will not cut down on urinary losses as much as they might, and the intestine will not absorb calcium from food as efficiently as it might, simply because the bone is responding more "generously" to PTH. But under such circumstances the adaptation to a low-calcium diet is poor; urinary loss is inadequately reduced, intestinal absorption is inadequately increased, and bones are torn down to meet internal calcium needs. It is like three friends going out to lunch regularly, with one picking up most of the tab, most of the time.

Alternatively, if the bones are relatively resistant to PTH—"stingy", as it were—then the parathyroid glands have to produce more PTH, which forces better absorption from the diet and better conservation by the kidneys, and the bones are protected. As we saw earlier, they are still at risk, but they get saved till last.

Do such differences in bone responsiveness really exist? Two examples will show their effects.

First, it has been learned only recently that the bones of blacks have higher resistance to PTH than those of whites. Scientists believe that this is part of the reason blacks have heavier skeletons than whites—perhaps the whole explanation.

Second, at menopause, when women stop making the female hormone estrogen, there is an increase in bone responsiveness to PTH. Most scientists now believe this is the reason for the great bone loss in the months immediately following menopause. It is not surprising that black women, whose bones are more resistant to PTH in the first place, do not undergo the same magnitude of bone loss as do white women.

While it is good for us humans to be generous with our friends at lunch, good skeletal health is not well served if our bones are the generous member in the trio of bone, kidney, and intestine.

You can now see how these three factors influence one's calcium requirement. A person who can absorb calcium efficiently doesn't need to take in as much calcium as one who absorbs inefficiently. A person who can shut down obligatory losses, particularly through the kidney, doesn't have to absorb as much to stay in balance as a person who can't hang on to calcium. And a person who can do both has a very low calcium requirement. Finally, bone responsiveness determines how much PTH has to be produced, and thus how hard our bodies have to work to increase absorption or shut down losses. The interactions of other nutrients with the calcium in our diets are important precisely because they affect these processes. Some alter absorption; others influence obligatory loss.

The calcium requirement—the amount we have to take in every day to offset daily losses—is thus different for everybody. But, once again, that's where the concept of an allowance comes in. If we all get at least the RDA for calcium, the majority of us will get more than we actually need on any given day, and we will never be in a position of pushing our bodies to the limit of their ability to adapt. We would only rarely have to cut down losses to the minimal obligatory level, and we would only rarely have to push absorption to its highest level. It is nice to have such emergency capabilities to fall back on. But it doesn't make good sense to run an organism on its emergency systems all the time. That's what low-calcium diets do to us.

13

The "Natural" Intake
of Calcium

Primitive human beings, living in their natural state as hunters and gatherers, averaged calcium intakes of 1,500 milligrams a day or higher. This is two to three times the typical intake of civilized humans and is more typical of the calcium-rich diets most animals enjoy. It is probable that this is the kind of intake for which our human systems evolved. Intakes habitually lower than this value probably strain the capacity of many people to adapt.

There are two ways nutritional scientists have used to understand what constitutes good nutrition. One is to identify the disease caused by inadequate intake of a certain nutrient and find the intake necessary to prevent that disease. When this is done for all nutrients, and when the results are combined, the total is a good diet. The other way is to observe human beings "in the wild," to note the intake they are adapted to, and then to use that as the standard of good nutrition. The theory behind this approach is natural selection—organisms not adapted to an environment don't succeed in it. If a population has lived for thousands—even hundreds of thousands—of years in an environment, it will have established a kind of evolutionary equilibrium with that environment. This means that, on the one hand, the environment provides enough of everything to support the population and, on the other, the population has become dependent upon what the environment provides.

Thus if the intake of a particular nutrient is found to be low, and the natives are healthy by whatever standard we choose to apply, we can reasonably assert that a high intake is not required for health under such living conditions. And if the intake is high, it is likely that the population has become adapted to—and thus has grown to need—that high intake.

The potential weakness of this reasoning is the now well-recognized fact that not all mutations are either clearly advantageous or disadvantageous, and not all balances between an organism and its environment have been finely tuned. So, even if, for example, we were to find out that early human beings had a high calcium intake, that wouldn't absolutely prove the point. So, as we explore the intake available to primitive humans, we have to do so with some caution.

One reason to look into the "natural" calcium intake of primitive people is that several nutritionists have used it to support their claims that we need very little calcium for health. They note that dairy products are the major sources of calcium in a First World diet; that access to dairy products has depended upon civilization; and that the individuals of some races lose the enzyme necessary to digest milk sugar after childhood. They conclude that a high-calcium diet cannot be natural for adult human beings. Is a diet low in dairy products necessarily low in calcium? As we shall see, it is not.

There are several ways to explore the question of the "natural" intake of calcium for human beings. One is to study people living in primitive societies today, in situations as close as possible to those that prevailed in the prehistoric era, little touched by what we call civilization. The other is to look at the findings of scientists who have studied the bones of prehistoric people and the vegetable and animal foods available to them.

Ethnologists have studied about fifty groups of hunter-gatherers in Africa, Australia, Southeast Asia, and South America. These humans feed themselves much as free-living

animals do, eating what they catch or pluck or find. They do
not domesticate animals and they do not cultivate crops. They
move about from one range to another, taking what food is
seasonally available—which gives them a wide variety of
foods. It turns out that they eat a lot of wild game and an
immense variety of plant products, including nuts, berries,
fruits, rhizomes, roots, tubers, foliage, water plants—on and
on. The nutritionists cited earlier were right: these people
ingest virtually no milk or milk products past infancy. Nevertheless, their calcium intake is close to 1,600 milligrams a
day! (This value does not include the contribution of small
bones or bone fragments, which can easily double the calcium in such a diet. For instance, Kenyan natives living by the
shores of Lake Victoria, have calcium intakes of 2,700 milligrams a day, primarily from the bones of the small fish which
are a staple of their diet. Other coastal and riverine peoples,
who derive a substantial portion of their nourishment from
fish, have similarly high calcium intakes.)

Just because people living as hunter-gatherers get a lot of
calcium doesn't necessarily mean they need that much. Still
this conclusion does seem to apply to at least some of the
nutrients they ingest. One of the hunter-gatherer tribes that
has been studied lives in south-central Africa, where there is
still some room to roam, but not a lot. As the tribe has grown
in this century, it has bumped into civilization, and groups
near the boundaries have had to take up farming, which feeds
more people per acre than hunting and gathering. But agriculture provides only a limited variety of foods, even if it
affords a relative abundance of some of them. The result, for
the purpose of this tribe, has been nutritional deficiencies
unknown in their former, free-living state: As these natives
left hunting and gathering, the reduced intake of at least two
nutrients (iron and the vitamin folacin) tipped some of them
over the edge into deficiency disease.

The fossil record leads to similar conclusions. After the ice
ages—roughly 50,000 years ago—the human population
density in Europe was low. The people lived as hunter-gath-

erers, and vegetation and game were plentiful. Thus there was an abundant food supply to support a hunting-and-gathering life-style. Skeletons from these prehistoric people show that they were bigger than modern European whites (even with modern preventive medical care), and that their bone structures were heavier.

Of course, there were many other factors besides diet involved. The physical activity of the "natural" state alone could account for heavier skeletons. However, it is interesting that the fossil record shows that over the millennia, as populations increased and the environment began to be depleted, skeletons got lighter and smaller. Exactly the same story is revealed in the bone record of the pre-Columbian North American Plains Indians. When population density was low and food plentiful, skeletons were bigger and heavier, but when populations increased and the ability of the land to support the people was strained, skeletons got lighter and smaller. Nutrition would not have been the only factor involved in these changes, but it seems reasonable to consider that nutrition may have been important.

Yet another approach to this question of "natural" calcium intake would be to look at different human cultures today and see how much calcium they get, and how they get it. This is not as intrinsically interesting as the study of hunter-gatherers, because no human civilization has persisted long enough to allow the evolution of a balance between the environment and its inhabitants. Nevertheless, if cultural patterns were severely maladaptive, the group could not have survived, so there may be some useful information to be gained in this way.

Once again, dairy products are not a prominent feature of the adult diet in most cultures and ethnic groups today—especially not in the Third World. The Masai of East Africa are an exception. They are a pastoral people, and their diet consists principally of liquid milk—with typical calcium intakes as high as 6,000 milligrams a day. For most peoples widespread dairy product availability depends on refrigera-

tion (or at least a cool climate) and a good food transporta-
tion and distribution system. Further, as we have noted, adult
blacks and Orientals tend to lack the intestinal enzyme necessary to digest milk sugar. But this does not mean that calcium
intake is low for them (as it would be for us, if we were to
take milk and cheese out of our diets). Many Third World
populations get their calcium in interesting and—to Western-
ers—unexpected ways. We have already noted the importance of bones in the diet, both of small fish and small birds,
eaten roasted or stewed. Central American Indians mix lime
(calcium hydroxide) with their cornmeal to make tortillas or
other baked breads. Tofu, a staple of Japanese cuisine, is rich
in calcium because the soybean curd is mixed with calcium
sulfate. Southeast Asian women, who chew betel nuts, prepare their "chew" by mixing the betel nuts with lime. Peru-
vian peasants add a calcium-rich rock powder to a cereal
gruel which is a staple food and use a calcium-rich ash with
the coca leaves they chew. Some Vietnamese, especially pregnant women, drink a liquid prepared by soaking bones in
homemade vinegar. This preparation is so rich in calcium that
two tablespoons contain as much calcium as one cup of milk.
It has been estimated that average daily intakes in all these
non-dairy societies can easily reach 1,200–2,000 milligrams a
day.

Calcium intake is and was high for humans in the natural or
primitive state. And many cultures, with necessarily more restricted ranges of foodstuffs than would have been available
to a hunter-gatherer, have adopted practices that add calcium
to their staple foods. Of course this is not firm proof that we
can't get along with less. But the nearly universal finding that
the natural calcium intake is high does nothing to support the
claim of several nutritionists that we need little calcium.

14

How Much Calcium
Do Americans Consume?

The typical North American woman gets less than 600 milligrams of calcium a day from age twenty to fifty, and less than 500 milligrams a day from the age of fifty on. Only one in six teenage girls in the United States gets as much as the recommended intake of calcium.

Having obtained some notion about what our calcium requirement is, about what recent studies suggest we should be getting, and about what primitive hunter-gatherers eat, now we can see how we measure up. American calcium consumption has been estimated in several ways, but the two most widely quoted studies were done by the U.S. Public Health Service. Called *Health and Nutrition Examination Surveys,* HANES for short, the first was carried out from 1971 to 1974, and the second from 1976 to 1980. They are called HANES-I and HANES-II.

These surveys looked at many nutritional and health variables. Calcium was only one of them. They systematically sampled persons of all ages, rich and poor, black and white, rural and urban, and they drew their samples from different regions of the country. Their nutritional information was dependent upon people's self-reporting of what they ate, and so they contain inevitable inaccuracies; but they are the best data we have. Even allowing for a certain amount of inaccuracy, they tell a sobering story.

CALCIUM INTAKE – MEN

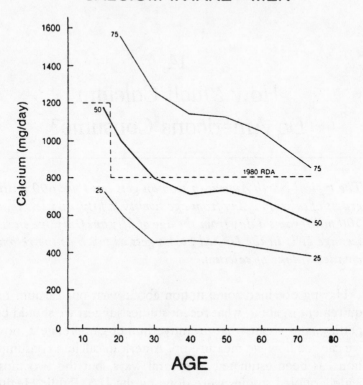

In the graphs, 25 percent of the men and women took in less calcium than the bottom line, 50 percent below the middle line, and 75 percent below the top line. The graphs also indicate the current RDAs for comparative purposes. You'll see that, while some men are on the low side of the norm, the median male calcium intake (the "50" line) is very close to the RDA. By contrast, the median figure for females hovers near 500 milligrams per day throughout the adult years, until it dips below 500 by the time of menopause. *One out of every four women gets less than 300 milligrams of calcium on a typical day.* Note also the low median intake during adolescence, when a young woman is building most of her skeleton. The RDA for adolescents is set at 1,200 milligrams a day, but the

CALCIUM INTAKE — WOMEN

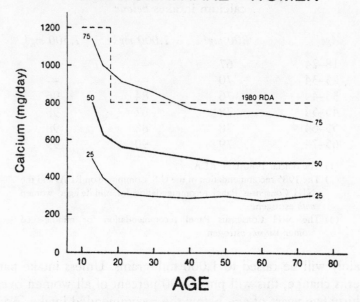

figure shows that the typical adolescent girl gets scarcely half that much. Fewer than one in six teenage girls gets as much as the RDA. It is particularly alarming that the calcium intake for adolescent girls was 10 percent lower in the second, more recent HANES study than in the first. This reduction in intake, exactly at a time when a woman needs calcium most, is a time bomb set to go off fifty years later.

The next table shows the percentage of women at various ages whose calcium intakes on a typical day fall below three figures: the current RDA; the 1,000-milligram recommendation for middle-aged women with estrogen; and the 1,500-milligram recommendation for women without estrogen.

These figures emphasize the magnitude of the problem. Young women (aged 18–24) do best, but fully *two thirds* consume less than the current RDA. Habits worsen with each decade, until by the age of seventy nearly 80 percent consume less than 800 milligrams a day. The RDA almost cer-

Percentages of all U.S. women with calcium intakes *below:*

Age	800 mg[1]	1,000 mg[2]	1,500 mg[3]
18–24	67	—	—
25–34	70	—	—
35–44	76	84	96
45–54	78	87	98
55–64	78	88	98
65–74	79	90	99

(1) The official 1980 U.S. RDA.
(2) The 1985 recommendation of the U.S. Committee on RDAs and the NIH Consensus Panel recommendation for middle-aged women *with* estrogen.
(3) The NIH Consensus Panel recommendation for middle-aged women *without* estrogen.

tainly will be raised to 1,000 milligrams. Unless intake patterns change, this will put 84–90 percent of all women over thirty-five years of age below the recommended intake. And 96–99 percent of all women over thirty-five are below the 1,500-milligram target figure of the NIH Consensus Panel.

By the way, we are often asked why teenage girls and young women have a lower calcium intake than males of the same age, and specifically why they drink less milk. There isn't really any one answer to that question, unless it is, simply, peer pressure. Teenage girls do not perceive that drinking milk is acceptable behavior—at least as judged by the unspoken standards of their peer group. Additionally, they associate it with parental supervision ("Now drink your milk, honey . . ."), and so they throw off this yoke with so many others. They are often excessively concerned with slimness and are unwilling to accept even the few calories of low-fat milk. Additionally, many young girls in high school and college athletic programs are given erroneous—and quite frankly very dangerous—advice by their coaches. For example, a coach might imply that heavy bones slow a swimmer down. Studies of nutrition knowledge among coaches have shown that their level of information about nutrition is very poor. Yet they often have more influence on a young person's nutritional choices than anyone else.

Once young girls break the habit of drinking milk, it is hard to reestablish—even though they may no longer be so tyrannized by peer pressures once they reach their twenties. Curiously, yogurt is perceived as chic by many postadolescent women who no longer drink milk. Yet fruit yogurts actually have more calories and less calcium than a glass of whole milk. So the choices, as with so many things influenced by fashion, are not entirely rational.

Boys, by contrast, operate out of a different set of peer expectations. Most drink a lot of milk, and their role models do too. So a boy who drinks milk isn't out of step with everybody else. Also, most boys burn more calories than most girls do, so weight watching is not of so much concern to them.

CALCIUM DEFICIENCY AND OSTEOPOROSIS

15

What It Means
To Have Osteoporosis

Osteoporosis is not a single, specific disease, but a condition in which bone mass and strength are reduced and in which fractures occur easily. The injuries that occur carry penalties of pain, deformity, disability, even loss of independence. Osteoporosis can involve fractures of every part of the skeleton—the spine is most common in the age range of fifty-five to seventy-five. After that, hip and long bone fractures become more common. Spine fractures compress the vertebrae and result in loss of height, stooped posture, chronic back pain, and difficulties in normal daily activities. Hip fractures, which occur most often in the frail elderly, carry a high death rate—about one in six—even though the mishap that causes the fracture is often trivial.

Osteoporosis is a condition, as its name designates, in which the bones are porous. Their external shape may be entirely normal, but they are less dense. The real problem with osteoporosis is that people develop fractures of various parts of their skeletons from minor injuries—so minor that they wouldn't even faze a person with a healthy skeleton. Osteoporosis is predominantly a problem of women. For every man aged fifty-five to seventy-five who has a fracture, six to eight women do, and after seventy-five 2.5 to 3 times as many women suffer fractures.

Over the last several years, many people with osteoporosis have written to us about their experiences, and our colleagues working in the community have added to this collection of personal stories. They show in a dramatic, personal way what osteoporosis means to some of the people who suffer from it. We let these people speak to you now in their own words.

> My back has become humped and my stomach distended, but the pain is not quite so bad in my back. Generally speaking, I feel very ill and weak and unable to do my usual housework, etc. . . . I have been told that I have a number of strikes against me . . . hysterectomy when I was 36 . . . allergic to milk. . . . Despite my handicaps, I hope to improve by taking medicine. . . . I shall be very grateful if you can possibly spare the time to send me information as to how I may recover from osteoporosis.

Stories like these are filled with poignancy, fear, courage, and resourcefulness. The people who have shared their personal concerns with us are mostly women, middle-aged or older, with advanced osteoporosis. They tell us what happens when the spine can no longer support the body. One woman wrote:

> At present I am suffering with a fractured vertebra. . . . I have had two fractured vertebrae before. I really can't explain how they happen, as I am very careful about lifting anything or doing too much bending.

And another:

> I have osteoporosis, and have recently experienced five fractured vertebrae. I have suffered terrible pain.

Yet another illustrates the fear of further fracture that afflicts many women with osteoporosis:

> I have played golf for many years . . . but am hesitant on playing more—since I feel fine now—for fear I'll damage some part of me.

The decreased mass of bone material in osteoporosis is surely one main reason the skeleton becomes fragile. We used to think that was all there was to it. We now recognize that the disorder is much more complicated.

Any bone can be the site of fracture in osteoporosis. However, some fractures are more common than others, and the two that have dominated both professional and public attention are compression fractures of the spine and fractures of the hip.

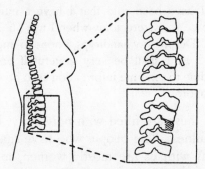

HOW VERTEBRAL COMPRESSION
FRACTURES DEVELOP

Typically, compression or crush fracture of the spine occurs when a woman is bending forward to lift something off the floor, to tug open a stuck window, to lift a heavy roaster pan out of the oven for Thanksgiving dinner, or any number of other ordinary tasks. As she bends forward, the front edge of one or more vertebrae is crushed in on itself. We show how that happens in the illustration.

Generally, if the bone is weak enough for one such collapse to occur, it is weak enough for several over a few months. This kind of progression is shown in a series of drawings from spine X rays of a woman who suffered a series of compression fractures over a period of several months. The compressed vertebral bodies are shaded, and each new evidence of further compression is indicated by an asterisk.

Each crushed vertebra usually produces acute pain (though sometimes spine X rays show many such collapses, and the patient doesn't recall having so much as a backache!). Typi-

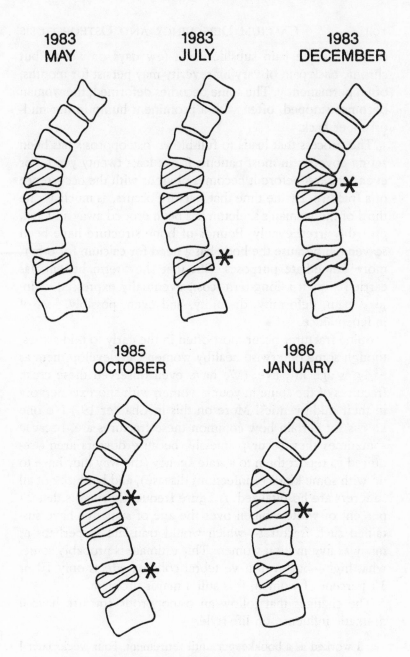

1983 MAY

1983 JULY

1983 DECEMBER

1985 OCTOBER

1986 JANUARY

PROGRESSION OF MULTIPLE VERTEBRAL COLLAPSE OVER TIME

cally the acute pain subsides in a few days or weeks, but chronic back pain of varying severity may persist for months, often permanently. The spine becomes deformed; the woman becomes stooped, often with a prominent hump in her mid- or upper back.

The process that leads to full-blown osteoporosis has been acting covertly in most patients for at least twenty years—or even longer—before it becomes obvious with the occurrence of a fracture. By the time that fracture occurs, as much as one third of the woman's skeleton has been eroded away and lost, probably irretrievably. Pounds of bone structure have been scavenged because the body has a need for calcium for other, more immediate purposes. But that short-term benefit has carried with it a long-term cost, eventually expressed as injury, pain, deformity, disability, and even, possibly, loss of independence.

Spine fractures occur most often in the early to mid-sixties, though some otherwise healthy women can develop them as early as age fifty-five. (We have even observed these crush fractures of the spine in young women with anorexia nervosa in their mid-twenties! More on this in Chapter 19.) No one knows for certain how common these fractures are, because sometimes they occur painlessly, because doctors aren't required to report them to a state agency (the way they have to do with some kinds of infectious disease), and because not all sufferers are hospitalized. A figure frequently cited is that 25 percent of white women over the age of sixty-five have sustained such fractures—which would translate to perhaps as many as five million women. This estimate is probably somewhat high—but even if vertebral collapse affects only 10 or 15 percent of women, it is still a major problem.

The changes that follow an osteoporotic fracture have a dramatic influence on life-style.

> I worked as a bookkeeper until retirement. Four weeks later I started getting back pain. I finally found out four months later that I had four compression fractures. . . . After six months I

felt well enough to go shopping, and carrying bundles gave me two more fractures between my shoulder blades.

Many women report that they are reluctant to drive or even to ride in a car, for fear that sudden motion will inflict further damage. They are afraid to hold their grandchildren or even "to have the kids over." The fear of falling may lead to life as a shut-in—perhaps more or less isolated from family and friends, social contacts and outside activities—especially during the winter months. There is the danger of being trapped by disability. Some women who have suffered vertebral collapse experience great difficulty in getting out of bed, putting on their hose, tying their shoes, and dozens of other humble activities out of which we build our independence. They find a hospital bed and trapeze arrangement the only workable solution. And for many, this also means that they can no longer sleep with their mates.

The other major fracture—that of the hip (technically, the upper end of the femur, or thigh bone) is typically a fracture of much older women. Each year more than 200,000 hip fractures occur in the United States, most of them in women over the age of seventy-five. By the age of eighty-five, one in three white women has sustained a broken hip.

While spine fracture can be extremely disabling, it is not fatal. Hip fracture, however, may be the precipitating event that pushes an older woman down the slide to disability, dependence, and death. In the United States, between 12 and 20 percent of hip fractures in older persons are followed by death within three months. However, it is not entirely fair to attribute all of these deaths to osteoporosis. Many of these fractures occur in extremely fragile people of advanced age, some of whom are already near death. Thus, it is misleading to say—as some experts have—that there are 40,000 osteoporosis-related deaths in the United States each year. We guess the number to be closer to 20,000.

That is not to say that the problem is not serious. Quite the contrary. It is sufficiently serious that its statistics are impressive without exaggeration. In the long run we believe that the cause of osteoporosis will not be well served by overstating the case. Quite clearly, hip fracture can seriously impair the independence of an elderly person and even lead to institutionalization.

Why do the bones break in osteoporosis? There are three reasons: reduced bone mass, poor bone quality, and a fall or other mishap that applies force to fragile structures.

Reduced bone mass is the technical definition of osteoporosis. Virtually every study of patients with hip and spine fracture has shown that those with fractures have low bone mass. Other things being equal, a structure containing less bone material will be mechanically weaker than one containing more. But other things are not always equal. Many people lose bone with age; many lose a lot; but not all of them suffer fractures. Some persons with fractures have substantially more bone than others without fractures. Why some persons develop fractures and others don't has become an important question. In recent years, attention has turned to the other two contributing causes.

We don't know for certain that people with fractures are more accident-prone than others, but we do know that women are slightly less stable on their feet and fall more in the home than do men. We know also that the home is often full of hazards: throw rugs on slippery hardwood floors, inadequate lighting at night, furniture to bump into in the dark, inadequate hand supports on stairs and in bathrooms, and so on. Shoes with narrow heels or smooth soles may be another source of difficulty. Some elderly persons are prone to blackout spells or fainting (such as when turning the head rapidly or rising too quickly to stand). Some drugs and medicines may make them clumsy or inattentive, and it is likely that drugs used to control "nerves" or sleeplessness are important causes of falls in older adults. Even getting up in the middle of the night to go to the bathroom can be hazardous. All of these dangers need to be considered if we are to minimize the risk of a potentially devastating fracture in a fragile but independent elderly individual.

The last contributor to the fracture problem is what we call poor bone quality. Either the bone material is defective or its architecture or structural arrangement is poor. As a result, the bone is prone to failure. These qualitative defects in bone material make it a good deal weaker than its mass alone would suggest. One way that bones develop defective material is when the effects of everyday wear and tear aren't repaired. For reasons we don't understand, the repair process can be so slow or ineffective that it allows damage to remain unrepaired for long periods. In some cases this problem may even be entirely separate from the reduction in bone density. But in other cases reduced bone mass and sluggish repair are clearly linked. Our bones normally "give" or bend a little in ordinary physical activity. And light, fragile bones bend and twist more than do heavy, dense ones. The number of microscopic cracks that constitute microdamage increases as the amount of bending and twisting increases, so they accumulate faster in people with reduced bone mass, and they demand a vigorous repair process. But in many older persons, the repair process is sluggish. So reduced bone mass places them at increased risk for two reasons, not just one.

Bone has what we call "ineffective bone architecture" when it has lost too many of its internal cross-braces. (You will recall that bone is a honeycomb of bony plates, most vertical but others interlacing with the vertical ones and bracing the entire structure. These cross-braces make the bone stiff and give it the most strength for the least weight.) Recent studies of people with vertebral compression (or crush) fractures have shown a loss of these cross-bracing plates. Other persons, with exactly the same reduction in bone mass but without fractures, have bone which still retains the system of cross-braces (though all the structures are thin). Clearly, for the same amount of bone, a good architectural system of cross-braces results in a mechanically stronger structure.

So bones are fragile in osteoporosis because the bone mass

is reduced and the bones are no longer well constructed. These fragile bones break when force is applied to them in a fall or other mishap.

16

Calcium and Osteoporosis: Prevention and Treatment

Low-calcium diets regularly produce osteoporosis in laboratory animals. But calcium-deficient diets are not the only cause of osteoporosis—just as iron-deficient diets are not the only cause of anemia. However, there is solid evidence that some of the bone loss that occurs in middle age can be attributed to inadequate calcium intake, to decreased utilization of dietary calcium—or to both. Calcium has a role in both the cause and the treatment of osteoporosis.

The work from our laboratory at Creighton first solidly established the link between calcium and bone health in middle-aged women, and our numbers for recommended calcium intakes were adapted by the NIH Consensus Panel on Osteoporosis 1984. So over the past several years I have become identified as "Dr. Calcium." Actually, that is a kind of stereotyping that I find uncongenial. For, while I believe calcium to be important for bone health in the adult, I also know that it is not the only important factor.

Osteoporosis is a complex disorder of bone quantity, bone quality, and propensity to injury. So far as anyone knows, the intake of calcium has nothing to do with the likelihood of falling. Nor do we have reason to believe that a high calcium intake will make anyone more alert, better coordinated, or less clumsy. Calcium intake also seems to have nothing to do with the process by which damaged bony material is detected and repaired. So these aspects of osteoporosis are not influenced by how much calcium we have in our diets.

But calcium intake clearly does influence bone mass. We know with considerable certainty that low calcium intake can cause low bone mass. But even here we know that calcium deficiency is not the only cause of low bone mass. For example, calcium intake won't prevent or reverse the bone loss that results from immobilization or inactivity. Also, there is typically a rapid loss of bone from most or all parts of the skeleton in the first few years after menopause. We now recognize that at least some of this loss is due to the fall in estrogen production and that it cannot be prevented by even large calcium supplements. Further, some skeletal regions seem to be more sensitive than others, both to varying calcium intakes and to estrogen.

So, while calcium remains a crucial nutrient, there are limits to what it can do. In explaining both the importance of calcium and the limits on what calcium can do to prevent osteoporosis, it is helpful to make a comparison with iron and anemia. Anemia is a reduction in the total amount of hemoglobin circulating in the bloodstream. (Hemoglobin is the substance packaged in the red blood cells that carries oxygen to the tissues.) Iron is an essential part of the hemoglobin molecule. Iron-deficiency anemia develops if the diet doesn't contain enough iron to support growth or to compensate for ordinary losses. Iron-deficiency anemia may also occur because of bleeding, for example when menstrual bleeding is prolonged and heavy. But anemias completely unrelated to iron also occur: anemias due to certain vitamin deficiencies (folacin or vitamin B_{12}), anemias due to defects in the metabolic machinery of the red blood cells, anemias due to crowding of the bone marrow by malignant cells (as in leukemia), and on and on. Of the many kinds of anemia, increased iron intake is likely to help only those due to inadequate iron intake. Does that mean that iron is unimportant? Hardly! In fact, one of every four cases of anemia is due to iron deficiency.

The relationship between calcium and osteoporosis is of exactly the same sort. As anemia is a reduction in the total mass of hemoglobin, so osteoporosis is a reduction in the total mass of bone. Some of that reduction may be due to decreased calcium intake, some to excessive calcium loss, some to inactivity, some to estrogen loss, some to drugs, and some to diseases or their treatments. Some may even be due to deficiency of other nutrients (see Chapter 17). Medical science does not yet know for certain what fraction of all cases of osteoporosis may be due to calcium deficiency, but available evidence suggests that it is substantial.

We know that calcium *does* play a role in building optimal bone mass during the growth years, in maintaining bone mass during midlife and aging, and in treating reduced bone mass and/or osteoporosis. Let's look at each of these roles.

THE ROLE OF CALCIUM IN BUILDING OPTIMAL BONE MASS

Developing optimal bone mass is probably the most important of calcium's three roles. The amount of calcium we consume during the teens and twenties determines to a great extent how much bone is accumulated by age thirty-five, the approximate age of peak bone mass. A study of this link was carried out in Yugoslavia. A group of scientists compared bone mass and fracture rate in the people of two rural districts. In one, the people kept goats and so had goat's milk and cheese in their diet. In the other, they did not. People in the first district had about twice the daily calcium intake of people in the second. Interestingly, the calcium intake in the high-calcium district was at about the level recommended by the 1984 NIH Consensus Panel; while calcium intake in the low-calcium district was close to the average intake of U.S. women according to the HANES studies.

What did the researchers find? The graph shows bone

YUGOSLAV DATA ON BONE MASS IN HIGH AND LOW CALCIUM INTAKE REGIONS

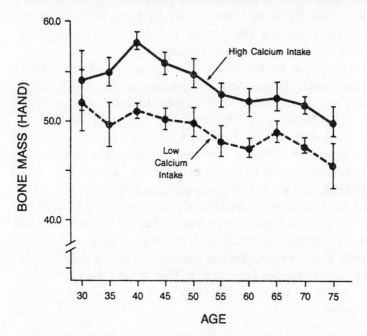

mass, measured in the hand, for the two groups. People in the high-calcium district had denser bones than people in the low-calcium district. This was true for every age, even for individuals in their twenties and thirties. This study strongly suggests that a low calcium intake—in other words, a calcium intake typical of adolescent girls and adult women in our society today—does *not* support the building of an optimal bone mass. The genetic potential for bone mass cannot be reached. The bones of young and middle-aged individuals will not be as healthy and strong as they could have been. And then, when age-related bone loss starts, it begins from a lower peak. Some of the reserves of bone that might have provided a cushion against postmenopausal loss will never have been there in the first place.

The graph also shows that older persons in both groups had less bone than those who were younger. But even so, at age seventy-five persons living in the high-calcium district had as much bone as persons forty years younger in the low-calcium district! So it helps greatly to have built up more bone before starting the downhill slide of bone mass that seems inevitably to accompany aging.

Several other studies point to the same conclusion. Each has compared bone mass measurements in middle-aged women against information about their lifelong—and particularly early-life—calcium intakes. The studies published to date show that women with high intakes early in life have more bone at midlife than women whose intakes were low. More research needs to be done, but these findings fit in with everything else we know about calcium and bone.

For all these reasons we strongly recommend that steps be taken to assure a high calcium intake during adolescence and right on through the twenties, especially for girls and young women. From everything we know, this is the best bet to prevent osteoporosis later in life. This is why the falling calcium intake of today's adolescent girls is creating a ticking time bomb.

THE ROLE OF CALCIUM IN MAINTAINING BONE MASS

Does calcium have any role in maintaining the bone mass we have managed to build, or at least what we have left at the age we become aware of the importance of calcium? The answer is a qualified "yes." We don't understand all the reasons why bone loss occurs as we grow older. Some of this loss is certainly due to decreased physical activity and to increased gracefulness and efficiency of motion. Some is due to a gradual accumulation of structural errors in bone, a decrease in growth hormone production, and an excess of thyroid hormone. It is almost certain that calcium can do nothing to stop losses from these causes. Recall that in the Yugoslavian study older persons in *both groups* had lower values for bone mass than younger persons. This suggests that some of the bone loss occurring with aging is not preventable by calcium.

However, we believe there is solid evidence that some of the bone loss in middle-aged persons can be attributed to inadequate calcium intake, to decreased utilization of dietary calcium—or to both. The causes of bone loss are like links in a chain. If calcium is not the weakest link in the chain, then adding more calcium will not make the chain stronger; it will still break at the weakest link. But you should make sure that calcium is not the weak link, as it is for some middle-aged persons. If your calcium intake is low—or if your protein, sodium, or caffeine intake is high—then you need more calcium.

You may have read articles that said calcium has been proved to be of no value after all—that estrogen was the only thing that can help a middle-aged woman. What are you to believe? First of all, there *are* real controversies in science. Scientists often genuinely disagree with one another. And when the subject is of general interest, the media exploit these disagreements and often exaggerate the controversies to sell newspapers and magazines.

So what is the story behind this controversy? There have been at least thirty-one large studies over the past twenty-five to thirty years that evaluated the effect of calcium on bone mass and bone loss in hundreds of middle-aged and elderly persons. Twenty-one studies showed that calcium intake had a significant effect. The others failed to find an association beyond what chance alone might have produced. Thus the preponderance of the evidence is on the side of a calcium effect. Any single new study—particularly a small one—cannot wipe out that body of prior evidence, cannot disprove the conclusion that all the other studies point to. Some of the reporters covering this recent controversy seem not to have understood that fact.

If there were many new studies, and they were all negative, then the balance would begin to tip in the other direction. But for every new study that comes along reporting no calcium effect, three to four other new studies show that there is one. Why don't the studies agree with one another? If calcium is important, shouldn't we be able to find that out once and for all?

One would think so, but science doesn't work that way. A recent study that was reported as showing no calcium effect is a good illustration of how this kind of confusion can occur. It was a study done in a small group of early postmenopausal Danish women. One third of the group was randomly assigned to receive estrogen replacement therapy, one third took a calcium supplement, and one third were given a placebo. Bone loss was measured at four bone sites over two years. The investigators found that estrogen eliminated bone loss at all four sites. Calcium helped at two of the sites but was not as effective as estrogen, and it was no more effective than placebo at the other two sites. The investigators concluded that calcium was not as effective as estrogen in the early postmenopause. They should have gone on to say "in women with calcium and vitamin D intakes like these Danish women."

But the average daily intake of calcium by Danish women in the age group that was studied is 950 milligrams, about twice the daily calcium intake of U.S. women. The investigators failed to consider this point. Why is it important? For two reasons. First, if your diet is already high in calcium, then chances are something else will be the weak link in the bone chain—so adding even more calcium isn't likely to produce much of an effect. Second, recall that the study was done in early postmenopausal women. That means they were all estrogen-deficient. But since Danish women habitually have high calcium intakes, relatively few of them could have been calcium-deficient. So what the investigators did was to compare the effects of estrogen and of calcium in a group of women who were notably lacking in estrogen, but not in calcium. No wonder more of them responded to estrogen than to calcium!

Does such a study prove—as the news stories tried to say—that calcium is of no value? Hardly. In fact, this study proves the opposite. Recall that, while calcium was not as effective as estrogen, it still protected against bone loss. That means that subjects averaging an intake twice that of U.S. women still were not getting enough to get the full protection possible from calcium alone.

So the long and short of it is that, while calcium cannot stop *all* the bone loss that occurs in the early postmenopause, it can stop some of it. We want to prevent loss of bone that is over and above the irreducible bone loss due to aging—bone loss that is due to calcium deficiency. That's why the NIH Consensus Panel recommendations make sense. They call for 1,000 milligrams a day for middle-aged women who still have estrogen, and 1,500 milligrams a day for those who do not.

THE ROLE OF CALCIUM IN TREATING OSTEOPOROSIS

To build or rebuild bone requires physical activity—work or exercise—as well as calcium. But if we ensure a diet high in calcium, at least we can be assured that a low-calcium intake is not making a bad problem worse or limiting the amount of improvement other treatments could be producing.

Osteoporosis is ordinarily diagnosed only after one or more fractures have occurred. Several studies show clearly that a high calcium intake can help reduce the number of fractures that occur subsequently. For this reason the National Institutes of Health—the federal agency that supports most medical research in the United States—has in recent years required that no new treatment be studied unless the untreated, control patients at least get a lot of calcium.

Also, we know from other evidence that certain types of experimental treatment—such as sodium fluoride—must include calcium if the regimen is to work. Fluoride causes a substantial increase in bone mass in many persons. But if adequate calcium isn't being absorbed from the diet, the body will take calcium from other parts of the skeleton and put it into the trabecular bone. It is robbing Peter to pay Paul. And we want to put more bone into the *total* skeleton, not just rearrange what's there.

For all these reasons, calcium is an important part of the treatment for osteoporosis. A daily intake of at least 1,500 milligrams must be assured. Many physicians want to push the intake for patients with osteoporosis still higher, to 2,500–3,000 milligrams a day. As we will show later, such intakes are still well within the safe range, particularly for the typical woman with osteoporosis, who usually absorbs calcium poorly.

There is one therapy for osteoporosis that is still experimental (and may or may not be approved for general use by physicians), in which a high-calcium diet is inadvisable, possibly even dangerous. It is calcitriol, the active form of vitamin D. Calcitriol directly increases calcium absorption to very high levels. It bypasses all of the body's natural control systems, leaving no defense against too much calcium in the extracellular fluid when high-calcium diets or calcium supplements are eaten. So a high calcium intake can be dangerous for a person on calcitriol therapy. The use of calcitriol requires careful medical management. So far as medical science now knows, this drug is the only exception to the rule about needing calcium in the treatment of osteoporosis. All other treatments, including those involving ordinary vitamin D supplementation, must include calcium.

17
Beyond Calcium: What Else Do You Need for Bone Health?

Building and maintaining healthy bones require dozens of nutrients. Phosphorus and vitamin D are the most important. Phosphorus deficiency, although rare, is associated with serious bone problems. Manganese, copper, zinc, and magnesium have been identified as essential trace nutrients, but their specific role in bone health is unclear.

Bone contains many things besides calcium, and the process of building and maintaining bone, like all body processes, requires dozens of nutrients. Whenever there is general malnutrition, bone growth and remodeling are impaired, as are the growth and repair of all other tissues. For most kinds of malnutrition, though, skeletal problems are usually less prominent than other problems. Usually, but not always.

One good example is phosphorus. Bone mineral, as we have seen, consists mainly of calcium phosphate, and thus it is not surprising that phosphorus deficiency might adversely affect bone in some of the same ways as calcium deficiency.

Phosphorus is generally abundant in our diets. But there are several conditions that produce a low level of phosphorus in the extracellular fluid—hereditary disorders called "familial hypophosphatemia" as well as ordinary vitamin D deficiency. Whatever the cause, low phosphorus levels in the body fluids do produce severe bone disease. The ordinary activity of osteoblasts—the cells that build bone—is abnormal, and unmineralized bone matrix accumulates at all sites of bone growth and remodeling. In children, we call this condition rickets and in adults, osteomalacia. These abnormalities are distinct from osteoporosis. It is not very likely that phosphorus intake plays a significant role in osteoporosis. But this example illustrates the point that nutrients other than calcium are also important for bone health.

Another good example is vitamin D, which is important for bone health in at least two ways—to facilitate calcium absorption and to maintain bone health by preventing osteomalacia.

Calcium, phosphorus, and vitamin D are the big three nutrients as far as bone is concerned, but are not the only nutrients that influence bone health. We have learned about some of the others from bone problems that have been observed in cattle, horses, and sheep raised on marginal pasturelands or fed markedly deficient rations. It isn't known whether deficiencies of these other nutrients actually cause bone problems in humans. But they might.

Four of these nutrients are worth mentioning—manganese, copper, zinc, and magnesium. Like many trace elements, these are essential for health. Without an adequate supply of the particular trace element an enzyme needs, it simply can't do its work. Manganese, copper, and zinc are important for bone health simply because they work with enzymes that manufacture the protein matrix of bone. Each has different activities, but deficiency always leads to stunted growth and skeletal deformity.

It stands to reason that manganese, copper, zinc, and magnesium are important for bone matrix manufacture in adult bone remodeling, too. Nevertheless, we do not now recognize deficiency conditions of these minerals in adults—at least as far as bone is concerned. We don't need a lot of these elements every day. They are fairly widely distributed in foods, and on a varied diet deficiencies would be quite unlikely. Furthermore, the body tends to hang on to these elements tenaciously.

However, not everyone has a varied and balanced diet, and some people may eliminate more of these minerals than they get from their foods. So deficiencies in adults remain a possibility. The most likely candidates for such problems are very thin athletes and women with eating disorders such as anorexia and bulimia. Many such persons have grave nutritional deficiencies sustained over many years. Many of them exercise heavily and perspire a great deal, losing trace elements in their sweat. Many also have serious bone problems, either osteoporosis or fractures that don't heal well. One well-known professional athlete—a man—ate an incredibly unbalanced diet and had serious bone problems. No manganese at all could be detected in his blood. This finding doesn't prove that manganese deficiency caused the bone problem, but at least it raises the question. And a recent study showed that patients with vertebral fractures due to osteoporosis had blood manganese levels significantly lower than people of the same age without such fractures. It is clear that a great deal of research is needed in the area of trace elements and bone health.

It would be a serious mistake to think, at this point, "Well, I'll just be on the safe side and take supplements containing the trace elements." Yes, we need a bit of them—but more than a trace and they're poison. We don't yet know enough to formulate safe and effective supplements of these trace minerals.

Magnesium is another nutrient in which there is a lot of general interest. There is a widespread perception among the general public that we don't get enough magnesium. One of the calcium supplements, dolomite, enjoys popularity simply because it is a mixture of both calcium and magnesium. What may be the basis of the popular idea of epidemic magnesium deficiency we can't say. Magnesium deficiency generally causes severe muscle weakness and incoordination, but it is not known to produce bone problems. Magnesium is widely distributed in most foods, and it would be hard to be magnesium-deficient without first having serious general malnutrition. In fact, the scientific committee of the National Research Council which is charged with setting the Recommended Dietary Allowances suggested in 1985 that the RDA for magnesium should be dropped entirely, since there was no evidence that magnesium deficiency of dietary origin ever occurs.

18
Use It or Lose It:
Calcium and Exercise

People tend to have about as much bone as they need for their particular level of physical activity. In fact, work or exercise is essential to bone health. Still, female athletes who exercise a great deal and who stop menstruating can develop premature osteoporosis with permanent bone damage. These women tend to consume far too few calories, and their intake of calcium is typically low. Starvation and hormone deficiency, not exercise, is responsible for their bone loss.

Calcium and exercise go together. They both build bone, and one won't work without the other. Exercise is the great undervalued component in building strong bones. Exercise and physical work directly stimulate the remodeling apparatus to lay down more bone at each remodeling site. This makes the bones denser and stronger, and thus better able to withstand the load placed on them. This is a system of beautiful design.

But if we are not very active, if we never place much load on our skeletons, then we will never develop as much bone as our genes would have permitted. Or if we were once active enough to build up the strongest skeleton possible, but then became inactive—because of a change in job or life-style or an illness—then the bone that is no longer needed is lost. We lose all that advantage. Not all at once, of course, for remodeling is a slow process, but in time the bone mass will drop back to a level consistent with the load we *now* place on our skeletons. That's why a lifelong program of physical activity is essential for healthy bones.

What kind of exercise is best? Some experts say weight-bearing and gravity-resisting types of exercise are best, but it is likely that almost any exercise—lifting, carrying, walking, running—is better than none. Probably the habit of exercise is more important than the specific type of exercise. "Habit" means building exercise and physical work into your daily activities: walking, carrying, using manual devices rather than power-driven appliances, and so forth. A life-style incorporating physical activity will probably, in the long run, be more effective in maintaining strong bones than will an occasional workout at a health club or a sporadic game of tennis or racquetball.

How does calcium fit in? Simply stated, if we don't have adequate calcium in our diets, or if we are not absorbing enough of what we do eat, then there is no way we can increase our bone mass. For where would the raw materials for the new construction come from? What happens, then, when a local bone remodeling site is being stimulated by physical activity to lay down more bone than it previously took out? How does the remodeling site "know" that there is not enough calcium to go around? It doesn't, for the calcium level in the extracellular fluid stays normal, even on a low calcium intake. The new bone takes all the calcium it needs out of the blood flowing past it, and lets the parathyroid glands worry about the problem (see Chapter 3). The body gets the calcium it needs from some other part of the skeleton —a part that isn't being exercised quite so heavily.

In one sense this is robbing Peter to pay Paul. But in another, it is another example of the beautiful design of the system. In the face of insufficient calcium, the body rearranges its skeletal mass so that it puts the greatest strength into the parts with the greatest immediate need. Still, it would be far better to get that extra calcium from outside the body, that is, from the diet.

So we need *both* calcium and exercise in order to have a healthy skeleton.

Now, what about the reports of bone problems in certain kinds of athletes, especially young women? Some of them develop severe osteoporosis—even compression fractures of the spine—these vigorous women in their twenties! Is too much exercise bad for the bones? No, that's not what's going wrong. Several important abnormalities have been found in these women. The first and most obvious is starvation. Generally the athletic women who develop osteoporosis have an extremely low body fat level—often 10 percent of total body weight or even less. (A woman needs at least 17 percent body fat for normal ovarian function during adolescence, and at least 22–26 percent during maturity.) Their daily caloric intakes range from 1,200 to 1,600 calories. That would be adequate for many people, but these athletic women are doing hard physical work. They're running an average of six to ten miles per day. That work requires energy—fuel—calories. Even at its most efficient, the human body burns about 800 calories doing that kind of work. That leaves only 600–800 calories for everything else. And that is starvation. The human body cannot remain healthy on that little fuel.

Scientists understand a lot about starvation. (It is tragic that we do, for that means there has been a lot of it around to study.) The body does its best to shut down all nonessential activities. It concentrates the available energy on maintaining life. And one of the first things to go is ovarian function. Women athletes with problems related to bone mass have very low estrogen levels. They generally no longer have menstrual periods. However, unlike with the menopause, their hormonal condition is reversible; when they put on weight, ovarian function generally returns to normal, with regular periods. Several such women who have been studied were able to become pregnant and bear children after gaining weight. On the other hand, it is not so clear that their bone problems can be completely reversed; and if they have sustained fractures of the spine, the resulting deformities are permanent.

Estrogen deficiency affects bone regardless of when it occurs: at natural menopause (at about the age of fifty), at the time of surgical removal of the ovaries (in younger women), or even in older women who stop estrogen treatment (often at age sixty or sixty-five). As we have seen, estrogen deficiency also occurs when starvation causes the body to shut down ovarian function, even in a young woman. The bone loss associated with menopause is really not a matter of age but of hormones, and it occurs whenever estrogen drops to low levels. It is clear that estrogen deficiency is a factor in the bone problems of these young women athletes. But by itself it is probably not enough to explain all that we see. For one thing, the bone loss develops very rapidly, much faster than what usually follows natural menopause. That may be partly because bone remodeling is normally much slower in older women, so it takes longer to lose bone. Nevertheless, there is probably more to it than that.

How about calcium intake? Most of the women athletes who have been studied have had calcium intakes of 600–800 milligrams per day—not up to the RDA for mature women, but as good as or better than most women their age. However, most women their age have estrogen, and we have seen, estrogen helps us to use calcium efficiently. That is why the allowance for estrogen-deprived women should probably be 1,000 to 1,500 milligrams per day. So the calcium intakes of these young women are more deficient than one might first think.

What about excessive calcium loss? That too is almost certainly a problem. During strenuous exercise the muscles cannot get enough oxygen to complete burning the fuel they use for energy. The partially burned fragments are thrown out into the bloodstream. These fragments consist principally of a compound called lactic acid, and this compound accumulates in the blood during strenuous exercise. It is later reclaimed and recycled (because there is still a lot of good energy left in it). However, some of the lactic acid gets eliminated through the kidneys and even in sweat, and when that happens it carries with it many body minerals, including calcium. Women athletes lose more calcium than a less active person would.

Finally, it is not just calories and calcium these women are short on. They just don't eat much *food*, and so they tend to be deficient in many nutrients—probably including some for which a requirement has not yet been specified. If magnesium, manganese, zinc, and copper prove to be crucial for bone health in mature adults, one can be assured that these semistarved women will be deficient in one or more of these substances as well.

One of the great advantages of a vigorous life-style is that it allows us to eat more, both greater quantities and more kinds of food as well. We thereby take in all the nutrients contained in all that food. We get the nutrients that are known to be essential. And we get nutrients that are not yet recognized as essential right along with them. It is ironic that exercise in some athletic women seems to work in the opposite direction. But the problem is not exercise; it is self-imposed starvation. Why do they do it? They are driven to *excel:* to be faster and better than others, and better than their own prior performance. When that becomes the goal, then pounds—and even ounces—get in the way. If they reduce their weight until their body fat becomes subnormal and then restrict food intake to keep it down, then, even though their speed and time may be good, their health is not.

Somewhere there is a happy medium. And at that magic point the bones will be healthy and strong—healthier and stronger than in less physically active people, as a matter of fact. In the last analysis, exercise remains a vitally important factor in building and maintaining a good, strong, healthy skeleton. And it is a factor under your control. We have more to say about exercise in Chapter 34.

19

The Problem of Anorexia Nervosa

Young women with anorexia nervosa usually develop severe osteoporosis. With markedly inadequate nutrient intake, the body shuts down the production of female hormones; sufferers lose bone just as postmenopausal women do. Also, the diets of anorexic women are very low in calcium, as well as other essentials. Virtually every woman with well-established anorexia has severely reduced amounts of bone in her spine. Though recovery is possible, many anorexics remain dangerously thin for the rest of their lives.

Anorexia nervosa is an eating disorder. It has been around for a long time, but up until recently it was rare. Since the mid-seventies, it has become an epidemic. Today perhaps one in every hundred women college students suffers from anorexia and many more from its cousin, bulimia.

No one knows for certain why these disorders have become so much more common in recent years. Psychiatrists believe that our society promotes extreme thinness in women in many subtle ways—through entertainers, models, media personalities, and peer pressure. Because victims see themselves as fat, they curtail their eating or try to get rid of the food they have eaten in an attempt to lose weight. The victims of both anorexia and bulimia are nearly all young women. In both, they think they are too fat—whether this is true or not—and they take drastic steps to lose weight. Anorexic women starve themselves, and bulimic women induce vomiting and abuse laxatives. Our concern in this book is only with anorexia, since so far as is known there are no skeletal consequences of bulimia (not surprising, as food *is* getting to their bodies, which are of normal to heavy weight).

Young women who are anorexic eat very, very little. At first they simply limit their intake, but later they lose their appetite and literally cannot eat much. Their weight drops to concentration camp levels. They are literally starving to death. For some it is in fact a fatal disorder. Experts currently hold that perhaps one in six anorexia sufferers die from this problem.

Young women with anorexia regularly develop severe osteoporosis, even to the point of developing spine compression fractures in their twenties. The explanation for osteoporosis in anorexia is straightforward. When neither nutrient intake nor energy stores can maintain basic cellular metabolism, the body shuts down all nonessential functions, and that includes production of female hormones by the ovaries. From a hormonal standpoint, young women with anorexia are no different from postmenopausal women in their fifties. More to the point, anorexia sufferers lose bone, just as postmenopausal women do.

But women with anorexia also usually have diets very low in calcium, just as they are very low in other essential nutrients. So at least for these two reasons, if not for others we can't yet recognize, anorexics almost universally suffer from severe osteoporosis. In our laboratory at Creighton, we and our colleagues have measured bone mass in dozens of women who are victims of anorexia. We have found that virtually every woman with well-established anorexia has severely reduced amounts of bone in the spine. Several have already suffered compression fractures.

Anorexia is extremely difficult to treat; nevertheless, it is not hopeless and recovery can occur. For those women who are successfully helped to regain weight, ovarian function will return (unlike the real menopause in middle-aged women, which is permanent). And bone mass will rebuild toward normal as well. However, if a woman has suffered spine compression fractures, the damage and deformity will be permanent. We know of no way to expand a collapsed vertebra. But the thinness of the bones, their fragility, the reduced amount of bony material in the skeleton—all the things that make up osteoporosis—can be reversed: studies of recovered anorexics show that they have normal bone mass.

But not all anorexic women recover. Many remain dangerously thin through the rest of their lives, and for them, osteoporosis with its resultant fractures is a virtual certainty.

Anorexia and bulimia are not disorders victims can handle alone. If you think you may have anorexia or bulimia—or if you are afraid your daughter might—you should seek professional help without delay.

20
Calcium and Oral Health

A lack of calcium may contribute to several dental problems. Both periodontal disease and the continued fit of dentures can be complicated by bone loss and jaw damage. Inadequate calcium intake probably promotes such loss. Tooth loss after menopause may be a warning sign of future osteoporotic fractures.

Unlike bones, teeth cannot remodel and repair themselves. They can be attacked by the bacteria in our mouths, and they can be damaged many other ways, but they can't be torn down to meet the body's calcium needs. However, the supporting bones of the jaws and mouth *do* undergo remodeling, and they can be weakened by a deficient calcium intake.

In the past, cavities and their long-term effects were the leading dental problems in the United States, but now, with widespread water fluoridation and the use of fluoridated tooth pastes, the cavity problem is a small fraction of what it once was. Looming larger now is periodontal disease—inflammation of the supporting structures around the teeth, with loss of bone and soft tissue and the ultimate loss of otherwise perfectly sound teeth.

Some scientists believe calcium plays a part in this problem, but the evidence to date suggests only an indirect, contributory role. Most experts believe that the cause of the problem is bacterial infection in pockets at the margins of the gums and teeth; the body reacts with inflammation and local bone loss. However, if a person with periodontal disease also has a deficient calcium intake and is tearing down bone throughout the skeleton to maintain calcium levels in the extracellular fluid, there may be greater bone loss at the site of the periodontal disease. That is, periodontal disease and calcium deficiency may interact to produce more jaw damage than otherwise might have occurred.

Something of the same sort seems to occur in persons who have lost several permanent teeth and need a partial or full denture. The fit, comfort, and function of a denture require that the bony ridge of the jaw retain the size and shape it possessed when the impression was taken and the denture fitted. Shrinking of the ridge causes major problems for denture wearers. What shrinks, of course, is the bone, and this happens by the familiar process of remodeling. And whenever we confront bone remodeling we know that calcium intake may be important. Although this problem has not been studied as extensively as it needs to be, there is evidence that calcium intake makes a difference.

In one study, investigators compared the calcium intake of denture wearers who had suffered severe bone loss in the jaw to the intake of denture wearers who had incurred only minimal loss. The difference was dramatic, with most of the severe bone loss in persons with low-calcium diets. In another carefully controlled study, a group of patients was given calcium supplements beginning at the time of tooth extraction and denture fitting. Another, similar group was given a placebo. One year later, the people taking the placebo had nearly twice as much bone loss as those taking the calcium supplement. Such studies suggest that even oral health depends upon adequate calcium intake.

Finally, tooth loss after menopause may be an early warning sign of future osteoporotic fractures. It has recently been noted that women who are found to have osteoporosis at the age of sixty-five report the loss of more teeth in the first five to ten years after menopause than do women of the same age who have denser bones. If this relationship can be confirmed by other studies, it could serve as an early warning sign. Dentists would be in a good position to counsel some of their postmenopausal women patients to seek advice about what they might do to forestall the onset of compression fractures of the spine and all the other problems of full-blown osteoporosis.

By the way, there was once an old wives' tale that "for every child, a tooth," reflecting the belief that to bear and nurse children a woman could expect to give up some of her own bones and teeth. Even if that saying once had a kernel of truth, it certainly is not true today. As we describe elsewhere, bone mass at menopause is higher in women who have had several children than in women who have had few or none.

21

If You're Sick:
The Effects of Major Illness
on Your Bones

Bone begins to waste away whenever we stop using it. Calcium intake has nothing to do with this kind of bone loss, which occurs whenever we are sick or injured or have surgery with a long convalescence. But when physical activity resumes, bone lost in this way can often be recovered if the diet supplies enough calcium.

Whenever people—men or women—are incapacitated for a month or longer by injury, major surgery, or some serious medical illness, their bones are affected. So long as they are immobilized or inactive, there is not much of a daily load on the skeleton, so the amount of bone begins to decrease. Remodeling begins to take out more bone than it puts back, and the bones become lighter and weaker. This is one more example of the body's adjusting its skeletal mass to a new level of use. This tendency to lose bone from inactivity has been clearly demonstrated in research in which fully healthy, normal volunteers were placed on total bedrest. These volunteers lost as much as 40 percent of the bone in certain skeletal regions—such as the heel—in seven months of bedrest. Such bone loss is the other side of the coin of exercise and bone mass. And in the case of serious illness, there are the added insults of fever and the outpouring of powerful hormones by which the body attempts to deal with the injury or disease. Both factors worsen the bone loss caused by disuse.

So far as we know, calcium intake has nothing to do with this bone loss, and calcium supplements will definitely not prevent or reverse it. However, when a person resumes a normal, vigorous life, it is possible to regain that lost bone in most cases. And during convalescence from serious illness, a high calcium intake is crucial.

In the past physicians have paid little attention to the bone loss that inevitably accompanies major illness or injury, and as a result have usually taken no special steps to support recovery of lost bone. We now know better. Both physical exercise *and* a high-calcium diet are needed during recovery. A diet barely adequate to meet the ordinary daily need for calcium may be adequate for a healthy person with normal bone mass, but it will not permit replacement of lost bone. Extra calcium is necessary if the deficit is to be repaired.

One or more major illnesses without adequate repair of the lost bone can significantly aggravate the general problem of age-related and postmenopausal bone loss. Although full-blown osteoporosis may not become apparent until many years later, part of the ultimate skeletal damage can be attributed to these earlier illnesses.

You don't have to wait for physicians to think about prescribing a calcium-rich diet during recovery from injury, surgery, or major illness. If a diet high in natural calcium is not feasible, this is a time when calcium supplements would surely be a good idea. Fifteen hundred milligrams of calcium per day should be about right. And be certain, too, that you have enough vitamin D. Often we overlook vitamin D during major illnesses. Then later, when we begin to convalesce, we are depleted of vitamin D and so have trouble absorbing enough calcium to repair the bone loss we have suffered. But, as we stress elsewhere, don't overdo the vitamin D. Too much is as bad as too little. Daily exposure to the sun is a good way to get all you need, but a one-a-day type of multivitamin tablet is an alternative.

22

Beyond Osteoporosis:
Cancer, High Blood Pressure,
Jaw Recession

For some persons, inadequate dietary calcium is probably an important cause of high blood pressure, and increasing calcium intake often reduces the severity of this health problem.

Some cases of colon cancer may be brought on by diets too low in calcium. High-calcium diets leave a lot of unabsorbed calcium in the food residue that reaches the colon. This calcium can neutralize the irritant substances that can bring out a latent potential for colon cancer.

When older persons have teeth extracted and dentures fitted, the bone in the jaw tends to recede. Denture fit may become a problem. Low-calcium diets make this problem more severe, and high-calcium diets help to minimize it.

The relationship of calcium to both hypertension and cancer had been studied for a long time before the media discovered them (just as the osteoporosis connection had). With hypertension the claim is that a low calcium intake predisposes people to develop high blood pressure, or makes it worse. Increasing calcium intake, it is held, will lower blood pressure. With colon cancer, the claim is that low calcium intake increases the risk of developing colon cancer, particularly in persons with a family tendency to that form of malignancy, and that high calcium intake can protect it. How much truth is there to these claims?

HYPERTENSION

Hypertension, or high blood pressure, is a familiar health problem. Like osteoporosis, it has been recognized for a long time, it has many causes, and we can do a lot to help, but there is still no cure or sure prevention. Whatever may be the specific cause in an individual, the underlying difficulty is a constant, abnormal constriction of the small arteries that carry blood to various tissues. To get blood through this increased resistance, the heart has to contract more forcefully, producing high blood pressure. Even so, some tissues don't get an adequate blood flow. Sooner or later the heart gets exhausted by all the extra work, or the artery walls, damaged by the constant high-pressure pounding, may give out and rupture. The result in most cases is heart failure, heart attack, stroke, or kidney failure, alone or in combination.

The reason for the constriction of the arteries is understood in only a few cases; in most persons there isn't a clue. Many scientists believe high salt intake may sometimes be a factor, but virtually no one believes salt is a major cause of most cases. Current estimates are that perhaps 15 percent of adults may be sensitive to the amount of salt (sodium chloride) in their diets. In the other 85 percent, salt intake makes no difference whatsoever in blood pressure. Nevertheless, the American Heart Association and the National Institutes of Health both counsel a reduction in salt intake for the general U.S. population, and at least one major consumer organization, the Consumers Union, concurs. That's because we don't know, and can't easily tell, who is salt-sensitive and who is not.

If restricting salt intake for the general population helps at least some people with hypertension, then it might be wise. But if it does more harm than good, then we ought to reconsider this recommendation and restrict sodium only for those who can benefit from restriction.

Recent research on calcium and hypertension suggests that sodium restriction may, in fact, be doing more harm than good. Needless to say, this suggestion has provoked a great deal of alarm (particularly from health agencies with clearly staked-out positions advocating sodium restriction).

Scientists have looked at large collections of nutritional information, such as the HANES studies, to see whether there were more persons with hypertension among people with high salt intakes. The relationship might be weak because most people are not sodium-sensitive. Still, with a large enough sample and the right analytical approach, we ought to be able to see a relationship if it's there. But we don't. What was found—completely unexpectedly—is that people with a low calcium intake have higher blood pressure than people with a high calcium intake.

A special strain of laboratory rats that develop hypertension from high salt intake has been used in much of the research linking salt and hypertension. It is particularly interesting that recent work has shown that these rats are even more sensitive to calcium intake than to sodium. One can protect these animals against hypertension with a high-calcium diet, even if sodium intake is high, and one can produce hypertension in them with low calcium intake, even if sodium intake is also low. Both these lines of evidence make it clear why calcium has forced itself upon the attention of medical scientists who are interested in hypertension.

No one has yet come up with a plausible explanation of how dietary calcium might affect blood pressure or how it might even protect against hypertension in some people. How can the muscles in the walls of the small arteries—the ones that are in constant, abnormal constriction—"know" how much calcium is being absorbed from food? As we have seen, changes in calcium intake have very little effect on the level of calcium in the extracellular fluid. Perhaps the calcium-regulating hormones communicate the information to the muscles in the artery walls. PTH and calcitriol are known to have many effects that have not been extensively studied, because they seemed to have little significance for the calcium economy.

That the calcium-regulating hormones may be mediating between dietary calcium and arterial constriction is further suggested by another well-known fact: hypertension is quite common in people who have a tumor that produces an excess of PTH. The same conclusion is also supported by a pattern observed in blacks. For any level of calcium intake, blacks maintain higher levels of PTH and calcitriol in the extracellular fluid, thus forcing better absorption of calcium in the diet and conserving calcium better at the kidneys. If there is anything to this theory linking low calcium intake to blood pressure, hypertension should be more common in blacks than in whites. And it is. Blacks in general have a lower calcium intake than whites, and osteoporosis is far less common in blacks than whites. In other words, they adapt better than whites, at least as far as their bones are concerned. But an increased burden of hypertension may be a part of the cost of this adaptation to low calcium intake.

No matter why, for some individuals, hypertension may actually be made worse by a low-calcium diet—just as sodium-sensitive hypertensive rats get worse on a low-calcium diet.

There is another reason that sodium restriction might do more harm than good. Dairy products, the principal source of calcium in the Western diet, are also relatively sodium-rich foods (180 milligrams of sodium in an 8-ounce glass of milk). So people who are concerned about sodium intake tend to reduce their calcium intake, too. Calcium reduction is not usually intended, and it is not inevitable. As we have seen, there are many other sources of calcium among foods, and of course calcium supplements can be taken. But the practical reality is that, for most people, low-sodium diets will end up being low-calcium diets, too.

There are many times when blood pressure rises in persons

with mild hypertension when they are placed on low-sodium (and hence low-calcium) diets. Then the physician may reduce their sodium (and calcium) intake still further, only to see them get still worse. Then they may be placed on multiple drugs with all their side effects, still achieving only poor hypertensive control—only to have the hypertension all but disappear when they revert to a normal diet containing both more sodium *and* more calcium. But these have not been carefully controlled studies, and it would be a serious mistake to leap to conclusions too soon. Nevertheless, such experiences do reinforce the notion that, for at least some individuals, calcium intake may be critical in the control of hypertension. It is clear that much more research needs to be done.

Hypertension is an immensely complicated problem. It is far too early to say for certain how calcium relates to it. But enough information has been accumulating the past few years to indicate that calcium has a role to play for at least some people with this disorder. We would hazard that there is a group of people who, given a high-calcium diet, would probably not usually develop hypertension, but would do so on a low-calcium diet. By contrast, other individuals develop high blood pressure for other reasons, and their hypertension is not influenced by calcium intake. Also, there probably is a truly sodium-sensitive group with hypertension, and whether they include some of those who are calcium-sensitive is uncertain. But it seems both safe and prudent to urge people with restricted sodium intake to make a particular effort to get an adequate, perhaps even high, calcium intake. This is one situation that probably calls for the use of calcium supplements.

COLON CANCER

Cancer, like hypertension and osteoporosis, has many causes. In many cases scientists believe that there are genes that under certain conditions become active and result in the unrestrained, abnormal cell growth that characterizes cancer. One of those trigger conditions seems to be cell proliferation. We have known for at least fifty years that some types of cancers don't occur in tissues unless cells are dividing. So scientists have looked for substances—such as irritants—that lead to unnecessary cell division.

With regard to cancer of the colon, or large intestine, the question was, "What in our diets might be responsible for unnecessary irritation of the cells lining the colon?" For people who have inherited a tendency for colon cancer, such irritation might activate it. A possibility considered by some scientists was unabsorbed free fatty acids in the food residues reaching the colon. Most of the fat in our diets consists of compounds made up of three molecules of fatty acid combined with a single molecule of glycerol to form what chemists call a "triglyceride." In digestion, intestinal enzymes split this combination molecule into its components and absorb them. But if the diet is high in fat, some of the fatty acids released in digestion may get past the absorptive sites in the small intestine and end up in the colon. That's wasted nutrition, in a sense, but still it does occur to a limited extent. The theory was that these unabsorbed fatty acids might irritate the colon lining. When this idea was tested in laboratory animals, it proved to be true.

Calcium comes into the picture because it naturally binds with fatty acids. It neutralizes them, in a sense. (The ring in the bathtub comes from calcium in hard water combining with the fatty acids in soap.) Scientists reasoned that an excess of calcium would bind the unabsorbed fatty acids and render them nonirritating. When this approach was tried in laboratory animals, it worked precisely as predicted.

In our modern diet, the amount of calcium reaching the colon is low and the amount of fatty acids, high, in comparison to the diets of our primitive ancestors. Thus, the theory goes, things have reached a point where there is no longer enough calcium left in the food residues to combine with and neutralize all of the irritants left over from a diet high in fat.

Chemical analyses of feces in fact show that this is exactly the situation for many people.

This group of theories and findings offers promise of dietary prevention of at least one form of cancer. But so far there is no evidence that high-calcium diets have prevented even one case of cancer in humans. The abnormal cell proliferation in the colon lining of persons with a family history of colon cancer has been reversed with calcium supplements, and calcium works well enough in experimental animals. But neither of these findings is the same thing as preventing human cancer. Again, we need more research.

JAW RECESSION IN DENTURE WEARERS

Another unfortunate consequence of adaptation to low calcium intake is the jaw shrinkage we talked about in Chapter 20. Some persons experience severe recession of the jaw ridge after tooth extraction, which makes it very difficult to maintain a good fit for dentures. Persons with a high calcium intake have less jaw recession and maintain better denture fit than persons with low calcium intake. The jaw recession experienced by persons with low calcium intake is not, so far as we know, a sign of general bone loss, nor does it mean the person has, or will have, osteoporosis. Rather, it is due to changes in the mechanical forces exerted on the jawbone during chewing. The shape and strength of the jawbone are dependent upon the forces transmitted to the bone through the teeth in the process of chewing. A full or partial denture transmits a very different pattern of forces than do teeth in their individual sockets. So it is not surprising that there should be some reshaping of the jaw following tooth extraction.

So why should people on low calcium intakes lose more bone from the jaw ridge than persons on high intakes? Why should calcium supplements protect against this loss, as they do? The best explanation is that persons with low calcium intakes have constantly high levels of PTH and calcitriol in their extracellular fluid. This is how they succeed in adapting to a low calcium intake. These hormonal changes force better absorption of calcium from the diet, and they push the kidneys to maximal conservation of calcium. But PTH and calcitriol are also potent stimulators of bone remodeling—specifically its initial, destructive phase. So, in a site such as the jaw of a person with recent tooth extraction, which is already marked for remodeling by a change in local mechanical loading, these potent hormones cause excessive bone destruction. It is a particular problem in the jaw because the process proceeds in a self-reinforcing circle. As the jaw shrinks and denture fit deteriorates, the denture wearer chews less, or uses the denture less, and so there is further unloading of the jaw, which leads to further bone loss and still worse fit.

The system, trying to adapt to a low calcium intake, seizes the opportunity to get some of the calcium it needs from the jaw in the region of the extracted teeth. But increasing the intake of calcium reduces the levels of PTH and calcitriol, and hence bone destruction. Ironically, the individuals with the best adaptation to low calcium intake are the ones most likely to suffer this kind of opportunistic raiding of regions of the skeleton currently subjected to little mechanical loading.

ONE CAUSE?

It is possible that some hypertension, some colon cancer, and even some jaw shrinkage after tooth extraction have the same cause—chronic adaptation to a diet too low in calcium. Recall that when the diet is low in calcium, the level of the hormone PTH rises, so the body absorbs and retains calcium more efficiently.

In healthy people, particularly young people, this system works fine, especially if the low calcium intake is only temporary. But if the system operates day in and day out at the edge of its capacity to adapt, then PTH and calcitriol levels will be constantly high. Much—perhaps most—of the dietary calcium will be absorbed, and the bones will largely be spared. But in some persons the arteries may be particularly sensitive to the chronic high levels of calcium-regulating hormones, and those arteries may develop problems leading to hypertension. In some persons the colon linings are particularly sensitive to irritation by the fatty acids left unbound by a shortage of unabsorbed calcium, and their colons may develop problems leading to colon cancer. While persons who have teeth extracted experience excessive shrinkage of the jaw ridge.

Such difficulties, of course, would manifest themselves first in persons who are more than usually sensitive to these factors. Something in their unique genetic compositions or in their internal or external environments makes them more sensitive to a calcium shortage than other people. That is always the case when the intake of a nutrient is pushed toward deficiency.

This is all very speculative. Nevertheless, this is how we put these diverse observations together as we try to make sense of them. This integrated theory harkens back to the concept of "diseases of adaption," introduced in the years after World War II by Hans Selye of McGill University. He believed that many modern diseases happen because the adrenal glands have to work overtime to help us adapt to stressful situations. The idea was quite popular for a few years but never caught on, and modern texts on endocrinology and metabolism no longer mention Selye's name. Yet the general idea of a disease caused by too much adaptation may help us explore more links between calcium and diseases such as high blood pressure and cancer. Adapting to too little calcium may have more side effects than we yet know.

WHAT YOU SHOULD
DO—CALCIUM

23

Computing Your
Personal Calcium Need

Scientific generalities are fine as far as they go. But by now you might be wondering just how much calcium you personally need every day. As we have been careful to point out, there are still many unanswered scientific questions concerning calcium needs, and for that reason we can't give you a hard-and-fast answer. Nevertheless, your decisions about what to eat can't really wait until scientists resolve all their controversies and complete all their studies. The calcium need profile that follows will help you deal concretely with the many factors that influence your personal calcium need.

The first step in evaluating your personal calcium need is to estimate your current calcium intake. (This is because some of the factors that affect calcium nutrition work differently at high and low calcium intakes.) The purpose here is simply to place your daily calcium intake—from all sources, both food and pills—into three broad categories:

Less than 500 milligrams
500–1,000 milligrams
More than 1,000 milligrams

The steps that follow will help you do this, at least in a rough way.

STEP 1. ESTIMATING YOUR CALCIUM INTAKE

Estimate how many times a week you consume each of the food items in the following list. Pay attention to the size of the serving. We have indicated common serving sizes; if your serving sizes are different and you want your estimate to be accurate, you must adjust your numbers. For example, our table shows milk in eight-ounce servings. If you drink four ounces of milk (a half cup) and you have one of these servings each day, you should enter your weekly intake as only 3.5 servings, not 7. Do the same for all the other food items. Also, don't hesitate to make commonsense substitutions. If you never eat macaroni and cheese, but do occasionally have a serving of au gratin potatoes, and if in your cooking you would use about the same amount of cheese in each, then count your au gratin potatoes as if they were macaroni and cheese. But don't count spinach—either raw or cooked—as a green vegetable, because its calcium is not available to you. First, in the blanks provided:

- Enter your typical intake of each food item (in servings per week according to the serving size shown) in the left-hand column.
- Using the multiplier shown, calculate a score for each food item and enter it in the right-hand column.
- Add the scores in the right-hand column and enter that figure in the box marked TOTAL SCORE.

ESTIMATING YOUR CALCIUM INTAKE

Food items and serving sizes	Your intake (servings/week)	Score
Milk, buttermilk, chocolate milk, 8 oz (1 cup)	_____ × 30 =	_____
Milkshake, 8 oz (1 cup)*	_____ × 35 =	_____
Cereal with milk, 4 oz (1/2 cup)	_____ × 15 =	_____
Yogurt, flavored, 6-oz carton	_____ × 20 =	_____
Hard cheese (Swiss, cheddar, etc.), 1 oz†	_____ × 25 =	_____
Soft cheeses (Brie, etc.), 1 oz	_____ × 15 =	_____
Cottage cheese, 4 oz (1/2 cup)	_____ × 7 =	_____
Ice cream, 4 oz (1/2 cup)	_____ × 9 =	_____
Pizza, one slice, 2 oz	_____ × 12 =	_____
Macaroni and cheese, 1 cup	_____ × 35 =	_____
Grilled cheese sandwich	_____ × 35 =	_____
Broccoli or other green vegetable, 1/2 cup	_____ × 18 =	_____
Creamed soup, 1 cup	_____ × 18 =	_____
Pudding, 1/2 cup	_____ × 15 =	_____
Baked beans or other dried beans, 4 oz	_____ × 6 =	_____

Food items and serving sizes	Your intake (servings/week)	Score
Cream sauces or cheese sauces for meat or vegetables, 2 oz	_____ × 9 =	_____
Calcium-fortified orange juice, 6 oz	_____ × 30 =	_____
Other calcium-containing or calcium-fortified foods	_____ × M‡ =	_____
TOTAL SCORE		_____

* Milkshakes come in various sizes, most more than eight ounces; enter your number of servings accordingly.

† Roughly speaking, an ounce of cheese is equivalent to a one-inch cube. Also, many cheeses are marketed in one-ounce slices.

‡ Substitute for "M" the figure given as percent U.S.R.D.A. per serving from the label of the product.

Note: You can check the package label of many food items—not just those fortified with calcium—for the percent U.S.R.D.A. of calcium for each serving. You can use these percent figures as multiplying factors for foods not shown in the table.

Calculate an estimate of your calcium intake from *food* sources (in milligrams per day) as follows: TOTAL SCORE: _____ times 10 divided by 7 equals _____. Round this number up to the nearest 100 milligrams.

Add to this figure any calcium you may be taking in *pill* form, in milligrams per day. You can tell how much calcium the pills contain by careful reading of the label. Please note that it is not the weight of the pill itself that is important, but specifically its *calcium* content. (You may also wish to refer to Chapter 25 for the number of milligrams of calcium per tablet found in several common supplements.) It has recently been shown that many calcium supplements do not disintegrate and dissolve in the stomach. Unless your calcium supplement is a chewable product or meets the disintegration and dissolution standards of the United States Pharmacopeia, supplemental calcium from pills probably should not be included in this estimate of your calcium intake. (In Chapter 27 we show you how you can determine for yourself whether your pills meet these USP standards.)

Please bear in mind that the purpose of this approach is only to give you a rough estimate of your calcium intake. If you want a more accurate assessment of your calcium intake, it will be necessary to keep a careful record of both the variety and the quantity of all the foods you eat for at least a full week. A registered dietitian should probably assist you.

STEP 2. ESTIMATING YOUR CALCIUM NEED

Some factors cause you to need more calcium, and others less. Still others, while important for bone health, work on bone directly and do not influence your calcium need at all. The following questions deal only with the factors that increase or decrease your calcium need.

Take a piece of paper and make two columns, one for the numbers to be added—labeled column A—and one for the numbers to be subtracted—labeled column B. When you have gotten through the questions, add up the numbers you have written in the A and B columns. We will tell you what to do with these numbers after you have answered all the questions.

ESTIMATING YOUR TOTAL CALCIUM NEED

1. If your protein intake is:
     Low (less than fifty grams per day), then enter 200 in column B.
     High (over seventy grams per day), then enter 200 in column A.

2. If your **Estimated Calcium Intake** is more than 1,000 milligrams per day, skip to question 5 and make no entries for questions 3 and 4.

3. If your salt intake is:
   Low (under 4 grams per day), enter 100 in column B.
   High (over 8 grams per day), enter 100 in column A.

4. If your fiber intake is:
   Low, enter 200 in column B.
   High, enter 100 in column A.

5. If you are more than 20 percent *under*weight for your height, enter 100 in column A.
   If you are more than 20 percent *over*weight for your height, enter 200 in column B.

6. Take the number of cups of coffee or tea (with caffeine) that you drink each day and subtract three. If this number is greater than zero, enter it here: ＿＿ times 25 equals ＿＿, and put this number in column A.

7. If you regularly take a one-a-day type of multivitamin supplement containing 400 international units (I.U.) of vitamin D, or if you get year-round sun exposure one to two times a week, or if you regularly consume three to four servings of milk every day, skip to question 8.
   Otherwise, if you have little or no sun exposure, enter 800 in column A.
   But if your sun exposure is occasional to moderate, enter 400 in column A.

8. Take the number of years your age exceeds 40: ＿＿, multiply by 15 and enter this product in column A (maximum: 300).

9. If you are *post*menopausal and are *not* receiving estrogen replacement therapy, enter 100 in column A.

10. If in the last ten years you lost weight dramatically because of dieting or exercise—to the point where your menstrual periods stopped—enter 500 in column A.
    (If you have made an entry for this question, skip to question 12.)

11. If you have had one or more episodes of major illness, surgery, or injury within the past two years, enter 250 in column A.

12. Add up the number of years since puberty in which your regular calcium intake was under 500 milligrams per day; multiply this number by 6 and enter the result in column A (maximum: 300).

Total for A
Total for B
Difference (subtract B from A)   —
Add 800 milligrams   + 800
YOUR PERSONAL CALCIUM
NEED   (in milligrams per day)

The range for which this questionnaire works is 500–2,500 milligrams of calcium a day. Estimates that fall outside this range should *not* be considered reliable. The reason is that the extra calcium you need for one reason will help you meet a need created by another reason. So if your calculations give you a number below 500, just call it 500 and stop there. And if above 2,500, call it 2,500 and stop there. Don't cheat on this! Intakes outside this range could be harmful and should not be considered to constitute your real need unless that conclusion is confirmed by a competent nutritionist who has carefully evaluated your own personal situation.

For some of you this will be as far as you need to go. But for others there are a few additional factors you should take into consideration, things that will affect the calcium requirement of certain women. For example, if you regularly use one of the antacids based on aluminum compounds (such as Amphojel, Maalox, Gelusil, Aludrox, and Mylanta), you should definitely increase your calcium intake, probably by at least 500 milligrams above the figure you have just calculated. Similarly, there are a number of medical conditions that may increase your calcium need. These are beyond the scope of this book, and should be discussed with your physician. Such conditions include sprue, pancreatic insufficiency, ileitis, colitis, and other conditions that may interfere with absorption. Chronic laxative use may have the same effect and create the same kind of need for you.

On the other side, some of the medications used for the management of high blood pressure may change your loss of calcium through the kidney—in *both* directions. For example, certain diuretics (called thiazides) decrease urinary calcium loss, and hence actually lower your daily calcium need; while others (such as Lasix) lead to increased loss of calcium, and hence increase your need. Once again, if you are taking such medicines, check with your physician.

And if you are taking anticonvulsant medications, such as Dilantin, you may need more vitamin D *and* calcium. Talk this over with your physician, also.

Finally, it is important to be very clear about the things that cannot be fixed by increasing your calcium intake.

- **Inactivity.** If you are inactive and get little or no physical exercise, you will lose bone. You cannot offset this loss by increasing your calcium intake.

- **Alcohol Consumption.** If you regularly average more than two to three drinks a day, you will harm your bones. Calcium won't prevent that damage. People who abuse alcohol usually have a low calcium intake, and for this reason may need more calcium. They certainly ought to increase their calcium intakes to prevent at least the added insult to their bones of calcium deficiency. But it would be a mistake to think that calcium alone can neutralize the bad effects of too much alcohol.

- **Smoking.** Smoking is bad for your bones, just as it is for your other body tissues. The bad news is that calcium won't help. You can't prevent the harm caused by smoking by increasing your calcium intake.

24
Is Calcium Safe?

High-calcium diets are safe. Many groups of people consume five to ten times as much calcium as a typical middle-aged North American woman habitually gets—and without difficulty. It is possible to abuse calcium, but a calcium intake of up to 2,500 milligrams is safe for nearly everyone. For most of us, there is a lot of room to increase calcium intake safely. We are better off to err on the side of getting a little more calcium than we need, than to risk calcium deficiency.

We are frequently asked about the risks of taking more calcium. Is it possible to get too much calcium? Is calcium safe? What would happen if you took too much?

The obvious answer is that it is possible to get too much of *anything*. In this chapter, we will explore what problems might develop, and how much calcium a person would have to consume to get into trouble. *But for most people calcium is quite safe.* More important, it is just about impossible to get too much calcium from foods alone. (That's one reason why we will urge—in Chapter 27—that everyone get the calcium he or she needs from foodstuffs, rather than from supplements.) To get too much calcium, a person would almost have to take very large doses of calcium supplements, or to combine large intakes with a drug (such as calcitriol) which seriously interferes with the body's regulation of calcium.

One way to get at this question of safety is to find people who regularly consume a great deal of calcium and to see whether they're healthy, and, if not, what problems they have. Data from the HANES studies indicate that slightly more than 25 percent of all boys and young men in the United States aged twelve to twenty-four consume more than 1,500 milligrams of calcium a day. That's about six million persons with intakes above 1,500 milligrams. About 10 percent of young males—or 2.5 million—consume more than 2,200 milligrams a day, and almost 5 percent—or 1.25 million—get more than 3,000 milligrams a day, the equivalent of ten glasses of milk! Moreover, since absorption efficiency is typically quite high in adolescents and young adults, these boys and young men are absorbing a great deal more calcium than a middle-aged woman would. This high calcium consumption has been going on for years, but so far as anyone knows, none of these young men has ever had the slightest difficulty as a result of this intake.

Similarly, prehistoric people and people living in primitive societies today have average intakes of 1,600–2,700 milligrams of calcium per day. Perhaps topping the list, the Masai cattle herders of East Africa typically have a calcium intake as high as 6,000 milligrams a day. Again, so far as anyone knows, harmful effects have not been seen in any of these groups.

Finally, there is a large group of people with chronic indigestion or acid stomach, who take antacids like popcorn. Although not all antacid tablets contain calcium, many do, and tablets of essentially pure calcium carbonate (for example, Tums, Chooz, and Titralac) are widely used. No one has accurately counted how many tablets most of these people take every day, and the number doubtless varies a great deal from day to day. But it is common for such persons to get 4,000 milligrams of calcium from antacid tablets alone, in addition to whatever they get from their diets. Again, there are no recognized problems related to this calcium intake.

Thus it seems clear that a daily intake of at least 2,500 milligrams, and probably up to 4,000 milligrams, is quite safe. (Incidentally, in 1979 the federal Food and Drug Administration certified the 2,500-milligram figure as entirely safe.) Since such levels are higher than most people get from food—or even from antacids—it is reasonable to say that calcium is essentially without harmful side effects at the intake levels reasonably achievable by most members of the human race.

What does it mean to say that a person gets too much calcium? If calcium were forced in faster than it could be carried away in the urine, calcium levels in the extracellular fluid would rise. If these levels get high enough, intercellular communication shuts down, muscles go lax, nausea and vomiting develop, and finally unconsciousness and death occur. But these changes are extreme and it is hard to imagine them happening just from taking too many calcium supplement tablets. Nevertheless, it could happen if other conditions are just right. We know of a 73-year-old woman who was taking 30 Tums per day on top of her calcium supplement. She managed to handle this huge load of probably 7,000–8,000 milligrams of calcium every day without difficulty until she caught an intestinal virus that caused vomiting and diarrhea, which in turn led to dehydration. Then, and only then, did her calcium level get out of control and she had to be hospitalized to get it back down to normal.

Some persons, who absorb less, can tolerate a higher intake; whereas others, who absorb more, could begin developing elevations of calcium in their extracellular fluid at lower intakes. Thus there is good reason not to push calcium supplements—if they must be taken at all—to high levels. We believe that, as a general rule, no one should take supplements at doses of more than 2,500 milligrams a day. Some experts recommend that no one take supplements in doses above the RDA—at least without professional supervision; this intake level, combined with dietary calcium, keeps the total intake within the range tolerated by adolescent boys, and thus would appear to be quite safe.

The problem associated with high calcium you hear the most about is kidney stones. There are many different kinds of stones which can occur in our urinary system, and many different causes, including infection, gout, and several rare hereditary abnormalities that result in urinary elimination of chemical compounds not normally found in the urine at all. But the most common form of kidney stone in North America and Europe today is one for which we don't know the cause. Such stones contain calcium and a variety of other substances. Calcium salts tend to be poorly soluble, and when the solids dissolved in urine come out of solution in the form of gravel or small stones, calcium is almost always one of the components. Those of us who live in hard-water areas have observed something similar in the water systems in our homes: the accumulation of small stones in the aerators of sink faucets or in the valves that turn the water off and on. These stones do not travel through the water mains; they develop right at the valve or spigot.

Since urinary stones contain calcium, and since urine does too, it has been natural to think that calcium in the urine *caused* the stone. It has been natural, also, to treat such patients by placing them on low-calcium diets. But it turns out that the reasoning behind this approach is not quite right. Most people, most of the time, excrete urine that has more calcium (and other ions) dissolved in it than is theoretically possible in pure solutions. The kidneys make a solution stabilizer that keeps the heavy load of eliminated materials dissolved and keeps it from forming gravel. It is, in fact, biologically important that the kidneys do this.

Water is essential for life, and when people work or live in a hot environment, the kidneys conserve water very efficiently by putting out very concentrated urine. But if the dissolved load of eliminated materials kept coming out of solution in the form of rocks every time we ran short of water, the ability to conserve water would only have gotten us, as it were, out of the frying pan of dehydration and into the fire of kidney stones. So ways have evolved for keeping that load in solution, even when there isn't much water in which to dissolve it.

The reason some people get kidney stones, it turns out, is

because their kidneys do not produce adequate quantities of these solution stabilizers. Calcium does *not* cause the stones. Calcium is in the stones only because it is in the urine. Having a lot of calcium in the urine can aggravate a tendency to form stones, but it is not the underlying cause. But if calcium in urine aggravates the problem, wouldn't that be reason enough to cut back on calcium intake? The answer is yes and no. Yes, if calcium intake adds a lot of calcium to the urine; no, if it doesn't. Generally urine calcium is not much affected by the level of calcium in the diet. In normal persons, increasing calcium intake by 1,000 milligrams results in an increase in urine calcium of only about 60 milligrams.

A few people absorb calcium very, very well, even when they don't need to. They have unusually low calcium requirements, simply because they absorb so well. Unfortunately, at high calcium intakes they are unable to reduce their calcium absorption the way normal people do. Something is wrong with their regulatory systems. Their kidneys must eliminate the excess that has been absorbed, and so they tend to have high concentrations of calcium in their urine. That in itself is not bad, but it does tempt fate. If their production of urine stabilizers happens to be on the low side, or if on a particular day it dips to low values, then they are more likely to get gravel formation than would someone with a low concentration of urinary calcium. No one can say for sure how common this problem is. It seems to be rare in middle-aged women. Among nearly five hundred middle-aged women we studied at Creighton University in Omaha, we found only two individuals like this, and neither of them had a problem with kidney stones.

Some physicians are aware of a disorder called the "milk-alkali syndrome," and they cite it as a kind of problem one can get into with a high calcium intake. Several years ago peptic ulcers were treated with large amounts of milk and large doses of absorbable alkali (principally sodium bicarbonate, or ordinary baking soda). Most of the patients did well, at least as far as their ulcers were concerned. However, a few developed other problems: elevation of the level of calcium in the extracellular fluid with calcification of the kidneys, some degree of renal failure, and calcium-containing kidney stones. In a few of these patients the calcium intake was so high that it could itself have produced the elevation of calcium in the extracellular fluid, but this was not true for most cases. Scientists now believe that the body's chemical balance was disturbed by the large doses of absorbable alkali. High concentrations of alkali in the kidney led to calcium deposits there. These deposits seriously impeded the kidney's ability to eliminate all kinds of surpluses and waste materials, including calcium. Thus, many of these patients could not satisfactorily handle even modest amounts of calcium.

Scientists now believe that the milk-alkali syndrome can be blamed on an excessive alkali intake, not on calcium. In fact, the syndrome has been reproduced in research by giving the alkali alone, without any calcium at all in the diet; moreover, it has never been observed by giving simply calcium, even at extremely high doses. We can confidently conclude that you do not have to worry about this problem as a result of increasing your calcium intake.

Finally, there is a worry we often encounter in talking and corresponding with people who ask our advice. That is the problem of calcium deposits in various parts of the body. A husband writes that his wife has calcium deposits around her shoulder, and her doctor has taken her off milk. A woman reports that her doctor has noted calcium deposits in her arteries, and has cautioned her to watch her calcium intake.

There are several factors involved in these kinds of stories. But one that is definitely *not* involved is calcium in the diet. A physician who recommends a reduced calcium intake under such circumstances is, simply put, wrong. Perhaps a few years ago, before it was recognized that calcium is an essential part of our diets throughout life, advising people to stay off calcium-containing foods was an innocuous enough recommendation. But not today.

There has never been any scientific rationale for the popular notion that dietary calcium can cause calcium to deposit around joints or in arteries—or anywhere else. Calcium has no tendency to form deposits other than in bone. In fact, the osteoblasts have to create special conditions so that calcium and phosphorus will deposit in the bone matrix. (See box on p. 25.) Unless the concentrations of calcium and phosphorus in the body fluids reach high levels, there is not the slightest tendency for calcium deposits to occur elsewhere. However, calcium deposits do occur at places where there has been damage to connective tissue. Calcium tends to deposit near the shoulder, for example, because bursitis, or injury, or some other problem, has caused changes that make the connective tissue act like bone matrix. The mechanism isn't understood very well, but we do know that it is a local problem, caused by local damage. It is not caused by diet, and it cannot be prevented by diet.

The quite common recommendation of many physicians to cut down on calcium not only fails to help the problem of calcium deposits, but it creates another one. It deprives people of the calcium they need to maintain bone health.

To wrap up, it is possible to abuse anything, calcium included. But a daily calcium intake of up to 2,500 milligrams a day is entirely safe, and has been certified as such by independent scientific panels in recent years. People certainly should not take calcium supplements at doses beyond that level on their own, though it is unlikely that they would get into difficulty until they took more than 4,000–6,000 milligrams a day. Finally, those few individuals who absorb calcium too well, and who cannot reduce their absorption efficiency as their intake goes up, should definitely not take calcium supplements at all, and perhaps should avoid large amounts even of dietary calcium. Even so, it is doubtful that they run much risk, unless they also happen to have a tendency to develop kidney stones.

Finally, what about persons who have a history of kidney stones? What sort of calcium intake should they have? It has been traditional for physicians to restrict their calcium intake.

But that is good advice only if they fall into the rare group that overabsorbs calcium. Otherwise, the restriction of calcium intake may create a bone problem in addition to the kidney problem. Only a few patients with kidney stones should be on low-calcium diets. With appropriate tests a physician can determine whether a patient overabsorbs calcium.

Calcium is as close to a nontoxic nutrient as one can find. We would all be better off to err on the side of getting a little more calcium than we need than to risk calcium deficiency.

25

How You Can Get More Calcium in Your Diet

The best way to increase your calcium intake is from food sources. Of the foods readily available in grocery stores, dairy products are the most calcium-rich. For those who can't or won't take liquid milk, there are several good alternatives.

We have seen that calcium is widely distributed in natural foods, and that people living in primitive hunter-gatherer societies can easily obtain daily diets with over 1,500 milligrams of calcium a day. But the question is: "How can North Americans choose diets with more calcium than they're getting now?" The tables in Chapter 9 will help you identify calcium-rich foods. The most straightforward way of increasing your calcium intake is just to try some of the calcium-rich foods and increase the variety in your diet. Inevitably, however, you will come up against the fact that, of the foods usually available to North Americans, dairy products are the richest and most convenient sources of calcium. And so our strategies for increasing calcium intake will inevitably depend upon varied ways to use dairy products.

If you want to increase the calcium intake of your family or yourself, it is important that you find ways to build calcium-rich choices into your routine food selection and preparation. That way you won't need to think much about calcium. Otherwise your calcium-rich diet will follow the same path as most diets for weight control, which are adopted for only a brief time; even when those diets work, they don't change the basic habits and eating patterns that got us into trouble in the first place.

One very flexible, convenient, and economical calcium resource is nonfat dry milk. You should keep a sealed canister or jar of it handy where you do your cooking. Here are a few examples of how you can use it. Add four or five tablespoons of nonfat dry milk to a cup of coffee. That makes perfect café au lait, and it gives you the full nutritional value of a cup of milk. Or toss a few tablespoons of nonfat dry milk into sauces, gravies, soups, and stews. It adds texture, body, and nutrition. You can also add extra powdered milk to mashed potatoes, pudding, and other foods that contain milk. Remember that, depending upon the brand, each level tablespoon of dry milk contains about 60–70 milligrams of calcium and fewer than 20 calories. Just calculate how many people you want to feed, and how much calcium you want to add in this way.

Grated cheese is another versatile and excellent resource for enriching the calcium content of the foods you prepare at home. A liberal serving of Parmesan on salads adds a lot of calcium (one tablespoon contains about 120 milligrams). Grated cheddar or Swiss are excellent for topping steamed vegetables, and they go extremely well in meat-based soups, stews, chili, and meat sauces. A tablespoon of grated cheddar contains about 60 milligrams calcium; of grated Swiss, about 90 milligrams.

When you're choosing fast foods, remember that some of

them can be good calcium sources, mainly because they contain cheese. Thus one half of a ten-inch pizza contains about 350 milligrams of calcium—more than a glass of milk—and even a McDonald's fish sandwich contains nearly 100 milligrams, once again mainly because it contains a slice of cheese.

What are some nondairy strategies? One that is available to anyone who makes soup from meat bones is to put a few tablespoons of vinegar into the pot while you are preparing the stock. This dissolves some of the calcium from the bones. Experiment with this. The more vinegar the better, but you will have to adjust the amount to suit your taste; it is best to start with a little and work up, because the calcium acetate that is produced by the interaction of the vinegar and the bone has a distinct taste. It is not unpleasant, but it is different, and you probably won't want it to dominate the other flavors of the soup. It is possible for a serving of soup prepared this way to contain as much calcium as a glass of milk.

This vinegar trick is inexpensive and virtually calorie-free. Other nondairy options are more expensive and many have a calorie cost as well. For instance, almonds, which, like most nuts, are high in calories, are also an excellent calcium source. They go well with many vegetables, casseroles, and fish. It would be hard to visualize regularly getting a major portion of one's calcium requirement from almonds. Nevertheless, every little bit helps, and among the nuts that go well with other foods, almonds come out ahead in calcium value.

Finally, look for fortified foods. Many food and beverage processors and manufacturers are coming into the market with calcium-fortified products. These products can greatly expand your opportunities to work more calcium-rich foods into your daily diet.

26
Milk Myths

*Misunderstandings often lead people to avoid dairy prod-
ucts. They worry about the cholesterol, lactose, and calories
in milk and other dairy products. Actually, dairy products
are low in cholesterol. Only fresh and powdered milk pose
problems for those who are lactose-intolerant, and low-fat
milk has fewer calories than many would guess.*

Whenever we stress the practical importance of dairy products, we are invariably bombarded with a series of "Yes,
but—" questions and comments. "Yes, but isn't the cholesterol bad for you?" "Yes, but what about lactose intolerance?" "Yes, but that's too many calories." There is something to be said for each of these responses, but there is also a
great deal of popular misunderstanding about these matters.

CHOLESTEROL

To the average person, cholesterol is a bad word. But that
attitude reflects a serious lack of understanding. Cholesterol
is essential for animal life. It is a part of the membrane of
every cell in the body. Cholesterol is also the raw material
from which the body makes the bile acids necessary for digestion of fat and many hormones, including male and female
sex hormones. So there can be no question about its importance. In fact, people normally make 700–800 milligrams of
cholesterol in their body tissues every day. This is three to

four times what they absorb from food. Thus, between what the body makes and what we absorb from foods, we get a total of about 1,000 milligrams of new cholesterol each day.

Cholesterol has a bad name because it accumulates as fatty deposits in the walls of arteries and contributes to the problem of atherosclerosis. There seems little doubt that high levels of cholesterol in the blood (above a value of 240, expressed as milligrams of cholesterol per 100 milliliters of blood serum—what is often erroneously referred to as the "cholesterol count") aggravate atherosclerosis. Moreover, persons with inherited abnormalities of cholesterol transport have high blood cholesterol levels and are definitely at increased risk for coronary disease. Clearly, cholesterol has a bad side.

In certain individuals, high blood levels of cholesterol can be produced by diets high in saturated (animal) fat. To control blood cholesterol, many heart specialists recommend a diet in which total fat from all sources comprises no more than 30 percent of total calories, in which saturated fat is low, and in which the ratio of polyunsaturated to saturated fat is about one to one. This is the American Heart Association's Prudent Diet. Dairy products, even butter and cream, actually contain very little cholesterol. A glass of whole milk contains only about 30 milligrams, and skim milk, none. (Contrast that with a single egg, which contains about 275 milligrams.) You can drink a lot of milk and eat a lot of some cheeses without changing your total cholesterol intake very much. However, whole milk, ice cream, and many cheeses do contain fats. The fat in dairy products is effectively the same sort as saturated animal fats. Thus, dairy fat both pushes total fat intake up and shifts the ratio of polyunsaturated to saturated fats in what many experts believe is the wrong direction. There are, of course, low-fat dairy products, such as low-fat and skim milk, low-fat yogurt, cottage cheese, low-fat ricotta cheese, and even regular Parmesan (which is lower in fat than many other cheeses). But most fast foods and convenience foods use other cheeses, so restricting intake to low-fat dairy products means cutting out most convenience foods. In these ways the Prudent Diet tends to lower total calcium intake.

What does this mean to you? Well, to begin with, only about 20–25 percent of adults have cholesterol levels over 240. For them diet can make a big difference. But for the other 75–80 percent—a large majority—it is very hard to change blood cholesterol even a little bit, even with the most drastic of diets. When we cut back on cholesterol in food, the body compensates by making more on its own, at least when blood cholesterol levels are below about 240. So it doesn't make much sense for most people to worry about the small amounts of cholesterol in dairy products.

Why, then, has there been so much publicity, even scare tactics, about cholesterol? Well, 20–25 percent of the U.S. population is a lot of people, and they can benefit by lowering high blood cholesterol. Unfortunately, we don't usually know who these persons are, and so the publicity has been extended to cover everybody, on the theory that it will reach the ones who could benefit from watching their fat intake, as well as those who really don't need to worry.

Usually that's a sound public health strategy—at least as long as the change promoted is safe. But there is a great deal of controversy surrounding the cholesterol strategy. Several experts maintain that the American Heart Association's Prudent Diet not only fails to be helpful for most people, but may be unsafe for some (for example, children). Still to be considered in the debate are the consequences of the Prudent Diet in the prevention of osteoporosis. The Prudent Diet essentially avoids all whole milk, as well as cheeses prepared from whole milk. While it is technically possible to get 800 milligrams of calcium a day while on the diet, it is quite difficult. Further, the NIH Consensus Panel targets for middle-aged women (1,000 and 1,500 milligrams of calcium per day) are just about impossible to reach while sticking to it. It may not be easy to resolve this conflict of public recommendations because a single answer will not do for everyone. But there are reasonable answers on an individual basis.

To begin with, the cholesterol problem is less common in women than in men. Women whose ovaries are still manufacturing estrogen, or who receive estrogen replacement therapy, are at much lower risk for coronary disease than are men. Further, the cholesterol in their blood, even when it is high, tends to be of a "safe" or "good" type. We know of no reason why the majority of women who are making or receiving estrogen should be concerned about cholesterol. Surely most of them should not worry about it as young adults, when they are still forming bone and need all the calcium they can get. In the postestrogen years, a different approach is needed. If a woman happens to know her cholesterol is below 240, she need not worry. (If you are in doubt about this, get your blood cholesterol measured.) Or, if she knows she is at high risk for osteoporosis but doesn't know what her cholesterol level is, she is very likely better off to choose a diet high in calcium, even if that means a high fat intake too. For her the risk of osteoporosis is greater than the risk of coronary disease. If she knows she is at high risk for both disorders (and very few women are), then the Prudent Diet plus a calcium supplement could well be the best strategy.

If you decide to follow the American Heart Association guidelines, it is important to understand that they apply only to *total* intake, not to *individual* foods. After all, a one-to-one ratio for polyunsaturated to saturated fat means you are still getting half your fat in saturated form. If you must restrict that saturated fat intake, you would be better off to get more of it in the form of dairy products and less in the form of meat. Women tend to consume more protein than they need, and less calcium, so such an application of the Prudent Diet is altogether reasonable.

The bottom line is that for most of us, and particularly for those who are most at risk for osteoporosis, the cholesterol dimension of dairy products is simply not a problem.

LACTOSE

Next is the issue of lactose intolerance. Lactose is the sugar contained in milk. It is a compound of two simple sugars, and in order to be absorbed it has to be split into these components. To do this, the intestine produces an enzyme called lactase and mixes it with the digesting food. All infants and children produce this enzyme—for, of course, milk is the natural, basic food of infancy.

Most whites continue to produce lactase throughout life, but a large fraction of blacks and Orientals cannot make much lactase by the time they reach maturity. They are said to be "lactase-deficient" or, more accurately, "lactase-nonpersistent" (for their ability to make lactase didn't persist). Lactase nonpersistence can create a problem, because the undigested lactose passes into the lower intestine, where it is fermented by intestinal bacteria, producing gas and often cramping, bloating, and sometimes diarrhea. Not everyone lacking the enzyme develops these symptoms, but many do. For these reasons, large amounts of fresh dairy products are not an appropriate source of calcium for many adult blacks and Orientals. For blacks this need not be much of a problem, for, as we have noted, they have particularly strong bones, adapt better than whites to low calcium intakes, and are not prone to osteoporosis. Orientals, by contrast, are susceptible, and for them adequate dietary calcium is critical.

Only fresh and powdered milk are a source of difficulty for lactose-intolerant persons. Cheeses create no problem, for the molds that made the cheese have already broken down most of the lactose. Even yogurt, which still contains most of its lactose, is usually quite well tolerated. The reason is that yogurt contains bacteria that themselves contain lactase. When we eat the yogurt, we digest the bacteria, too; they release their lactase, which then acts in our intestines just as if our own bodies had produced it. Also, several lactose-reduced milks are now being produced.

Actually, relatively few white women are lactose-intolerant. Much more common is the report "Milk doesn't agree with me" or "I am allergic to milk." Some seem to feel it increases sinus drainage or phlegm in their throats. Others are simply vague. It is hard to find an objective basis for these complaints. When milk or other dairy products are given to such persons under controlled conditions, they are almost always well tolerated. Still, such persons are unlikely to change a lifelong habit of avoiding milk when it doesn't "agree" with them.

Some children are taken off of milk during infancy because they are "allergic" to it. Many babies have feeding problems, but most of those problems are not true allergies. Instead, they have causes that are never fully explained, and most children simply grow out of them. Formula after formula may be tried, one food eliminated and then another, without ever knowing which food or food component was at fault, and usually without assurance that the difficulty was definitely due to food in the first place. By the time such a child is in school, parents ought to ask their pediatricians about the cautious addition of dairy products to the child's diet. If there turns out to be no continuing reason to exclude milk, it is a good idea to get it into the daily diet at a time when food habits are still being formed.

CALORIES

Many people say "Well, I like milk and cheese, but I just don't want the calories." Here are a few facts. An eight-ounce glass of 2 percent milk contains only 121 calories, and of skim milk, only 86. Compare that with a can of beer at 148 calories (even "light" beer is still about 100), a can of Coke at 144 calories, or a glass of orange juice at 110. And milk is more than just a beverage: it is a good source of calcium and phosphorus as well as riboflavin, protein, and other nutrients. For its relatively few calories, it is a great nutritional bargain.

We would be far better off to cut back on snacks, candies, and sweet desserts—where the calories tend to lack significant nutritional value beyond energy—and on fried fast foods.

27

Calcium from the Drugstore

Calcium supplements are a poor second choice to food. There are good reasons why it is better to get your calcium from the garden, dairy, or grocery store than from the drugstore. Nevertheless, it is better to use a supplement than to take in too little calcium. There are dozens of calcium supplements on the market, and they are not all equal.

"How much calcium should I take?" "Which calcium supplement is best?" First, you have to know what supplements are, what they are a supplement *to*, which circumstances call for supplements, and which do not.

WHAT ARE SUPPLEMENTS?

First of all, calcium supplements are basically chemical salts of calcium—Calcium exists in nature as salts, chemical compounds of positively charged calcium ions and some negatively charged ion that electrically balances the composite. Even the calcium we obtain in food exists as salts of one kind or another, combined with protein, with phosphate, or with a variety of complex organic molecules. Generally foods are chemically so complex that we can't define their precise makeup. But the calcium they contain is always there as some kind of salt or another, usually several different kinds in the same food.

Calcium supplements, by contrast, are refined, simple chemical salts obtained from natural products or minerals mined out of the ground, or even manufactured from pure chemicals. Several calcium salts are particularly common in the U.S. supplement market; others dominate other national markets; and theoretically there are many, many possible salts that might be used as supplements. The principal ones sold in the United States are listed in the table. The table contains the chemical name of the salt, some but not all of the hundreds of brand names under which these salts are available, the proportion of calcium in each preparation, and the number of pills one would have to take each day to provide 1,000 milligrams of calcium.

Calcium in some foods or supplements may be more easily dissolved than others and thus better absorbed, but once dissolved, they are all the same, at least as far as the calcium is concerned. However, there are special circumstances in which other nutrients may promote calcium absorption. Milk sugar (lactose) and probably other sugars as well seem to help absorption. How much difference they make in calcium absorption by the average adult is not known, but it probably is not great. Any claims advertisers or health food stores may make to the contrary are mostly nonsense.

One of the first things that strikes a person who looks at the chart is the large number of different supplements based on calcium carbonate. Calcium carbonate is extremely widespread in nature, being the stuff of chalk, limestone, pearls, and seashells. So perhaps it is not surprising that it dominates the supplement market, too. Nevertheless, it is worth noting that an antacid tablet, such as Tums, and an oyster shell preparation, such as Os-Cal, are basically the same substance. As a matter of fact, some physicians working in the osteoporosis field had been recommending Tums to their patients as a cheap calcium source long before its manufacturer caught on to the fact that it had another potential market.

CALCIUM SUPPLEMENTS

Chemical Form	Percent Calcium	Brand/Product Names	No. Tablets/Day to provide 1,000 mg
Calcium carbonate	40	Oyster-shell 500	2
		Os-Cal 500	2
		Caltrate 600	2
		Bio-Cal 500	2
		Calcium carbonate 260	4
		Tums	5
		Titralac	5
		Alka-2 Chewable	5
Calcium phosphate	29–38	Posture	2
		Di-Cal D	4
Calcium lactate	13	Formula 81	12
		Various brands	10
Calcium gluconate	9	Various brands	16–20
"Chelated" calcium	c. 10	Various brands	6
		Calcium Orotate	10–20
Dolomite	22		8
Bonemeal	32		5
Calcium citrate	13	Citracal	5

The supplement market in the United States has grown enormously in the last few years. Pharmaceutical industry sources say that it totaled a modest $17 million in 1980 and had risen to over $120 million by 1985, and they estimate that the market will hit $200 million by 1988. It is an extremely competitive market, and the consumer is assaulted by claims of superiority of one product over another. Miles Laboratory promotes its product (Bio-Cal) as superior to the oyster shell preparations because it is 100 percent calcium carbonate, and it draws an unfavorable comparison to the oyster shell preparations that inevitably contain traces of other substances. By contrast, several oyster shell manufacturers promote their product as completely "natural," as contrasted with "refined," "processed" calcium carbonate products. The facts are that chemically and nutritionally there is no advantage of one product over the other.

Most such claims are pure hype. Some are even downright silly. For example, one of the relative newcomers, Posture, a calcium phosphate preparation, was initially promoted—even on its label—as causing "no gas distress." The manufacturer said calcium carbonate preparations caused this problem. That was nonsense. We don't particularly favor the carbonate preparations over the others, but we certainly don't believe it right to accuse carbonate of problems it doesn't have. This promotional claim was silly on another ground; the manufacturer could validly have touted Posture as containing both of the minerals (calcium *and* phosphorus) needed for bone. Nobody knows how important the phosphorus is, but at least it would have been a valid claim and a plausible benefit. Why the manufacturer ignored the obvious and settled on "no gas distress" is a mystery, but in January 1986 the FDA ordered the manufacturer to cease this misleading labeling.

WHY FOOD IS BETTER THAN SUPPLEMENTS

Why take supplements? And what are they a supplement to? The purpose of taking extra calcium is to bring total calcium intake up to levels necessary for good bone health when you can't do this through foods alone. For instance, if a person were allergic to all dairy products and needed, say, 1,000–1,500 milligrams of calcium a day, it would be difficult to get that much out of other, ordinarily available foods. So in such circumstances, a supplement might be both appropriate and necessary. But supplements should only make up for what diets do not provide. *The natural and ordinary way to get nutrients is out of the garden and the grocery store, not out of the drugstore.*

We believe this to be a very important principle, and before we describe and compare the various supplements, we would like to list seven reasons why supplements are a poor second choice to calcium in foods.

1. *All nutrients are required by our bodies in balanced proportions with other nutrients.* As we have seen, bone mineral consists not just of calcium, but of phosphorus, too, and we can't build or sustain bone without both. Generally our diets are less likely to be deficient in phosphorus than they are in calcium, but nevertheless the need is there. Magnesium, manganese, copper, and zinc are probably also important for bone health. Even more important, other nutrients also important for bone health are doubtless still unrecognized. Further, there may be nutrients that help us absorb and retain calcium. Yes, taking calcium in supplement form provides calcium and maybe phosphorus, but generally nothing else. However, if calcium comes in food, it comes along with other nutrients too, even those we don't yet know about. And the greater the variety of our food, the more likely it is that our diets will include all the nutrients we need.

2. *Single-nutrient supplements can create imbalances of other nutrients.* Often, if a diet tends to be low in one nutrient, it is low or borderline in others as well. And when a single-nutrient supplement is taken, particularly in large doses, there is a risk of unbalancing the whole situation and creating deficiencies of some of these other nutrients. Nutritionists have recognized this phenomenon for many years, and are seeing more cases recently, particularly associated with megadoses of certain B-vitamins, such as B_6. Iron and zinc deficiencies can be induced in animals with large calcium supplements. Although this has not yet been reported in humans, the opposite effect *has* been found; a single-nutrient zinc supplement has been shown to interfere with calcium absorption in hu-

mans. So, with single-nutrient supplements, one problem may be solved, only to create another. The point is that even the experts don't know enough to manage human nutrition with pills. If we need more of one nutrient, what we need is *food*—food that not only supplies the nutrient we know we need, but supplies it in balance with other essential nutrients as well.

3. *We don't know the long-term safety and effects of the large doses of the negative ions that accompany calcium in supplements.* For every 1,000 milligrams of calcium in calcium carbonate, a person also gets 1,500 milligrams of carbonate. Is that amount safe? It probably is, but nobody knows for sure, and in particular nobody knows what its effects might be if taken every day for 10 or 20 years. And for every 1,000 milligrams of calcium in calcium gluconate, a person actually gets about 11,000 milligrams of gluconate! Is that amount safe? Probably—but, again, nobody knows for sure. However, when calcium enters the body in foods it is combined with a variety of negative ions, and you are not likely to have a high daily intake of any one of them.

4. *We can't overdose on calcium in foods, but we can with supplements.* Calcium is quite safe, and it is virtually impossible for a healthy person to get an excess of calcium from food sources alone. But supplements make it possible to do so. Inevitably, some people will take too many pills on the theory that if a little is good, more is better. Further, having bottles of calcium supplements around invites ingestion by children and infants. The flavor and form of some supplements surely promotes the notion that they are a kind of candy. Calcium is certainly much safer than many tablets found in the average household. But food remains inherently safer than supplements.

5. *We are less likely to be consistent about taking pills than we are about good dietary habits.* If you decide you need extra calcium, and you choose supplements, you will have to remem-

ber to take your pills every day—for life. Experience tells us that people often forget, or they get tired of taking pills and simply quit. Even persons with serious chronic illnesses, who need their medicine daily (such as patients with diabetes, hypothyroidism, or epilepsy), often rebel against having to take pills. Is it likely that people will stick with a calcium supplement from which they can perceive no obvious, immediate benefit? Hardly. By contrast, few of us forget to eat or tire of it. Just one more example of why pills are less reliable than food.

6. *Taking pills is more expensive than good nutrition is.* Even when the raw material in a pill is cheap (as is oyster shell or other forms of calcium carbonate), there are the costs of manufacturing, packaging, distribution, advertising, and profit. The price of calcium supplements varies, but compared with dairy products and other food sources, they tend to be poor calcium bargains, milligram for milligram. And with food sources, you're getting not just the calcium, but other valuable nutrients as well.

7. *The idea that the average person has to take medicines to be healthy is sick.* Medicines can be great for curing acute diseases (antibiotics for bacterial infections are a good example), but once you're well you ordinarily don't need them anymore. Moreover, there are no medicines that will cure a bad lifestyle. We have already seen that calcium won't prevent bone loss due to inactivity. If your calcium intake is low because your food intake is low, chances are you're not very active, and in that case calcium supplements will do little or nothing for you. You need more calcium, perhaps, but you need exercise or physical work too, and calcium alone won't be enough to give you healthy bones.

HOW TO CHOOSE A SUPPLEMENT

Now, if there is a good reason why you can't get what you need from foods, then supplements will be the way to go. While supplements are a poor second choice after food, it is still better to try to get the calcium you need from supplements than not to get it at all. Here are some guidelines to help you make your own choices.

Not all of the supplements on the market today have been tested for absorbability, and some may never be tested, so we can't say for certain how well each of them is absorbed. However most of the calcium salts that have been tested exhibit absorption values that don't vary more than plus or minus 30 percent from food calcium absorption. So there is very little basis for choosing among them on chemical grounds. But you need to take more tablets of some kinds of supplements to get your daily requirement. Superior absorbability helps, but it is rarely the decisive factor. For example, assume that calcium citrate is 25 percent better absorbed than calcium carbonate. (No one knows for certain, because not enough studies have been done. Some show better absorption for citrate, others no difference.) As the table shows, you have to take five tablets of calcium citrate to get the same calcium as provided by two tablets of calcium carbonate. Calcium citrate's 25 percent absorption advantage would lower the required dosage from five to four tablets a day—not much change. Calcium carbonate is still fewer tablets and probably costs less as well.

Similarly, though the data here are limited as well, calcium phosphate appears to be perhaps 25–30 percent less well absorbed than calcium carbonate, but in practical terms this difference can be more than offset by increasing the daily dosage of calcium phosphate by just one tablet.

The preparations based on citrate seem somewhat better absorbed than are, say, carbonate preparations, particularly if the tablets are taken on an empty stomach and if a person is deficient in gastric acid production. But most of this difference disappears if the tablets are taken with food. As we have just noted, the remaining superiority of the citrate preparations can be quite easily compensated for by taking a slightly larger dose of the noncitrate preparation. However, the calcium citrate preparations have one other slight edge on some of the other supplements if you have a tendency to kidney stones. The relatively large citrate load you get with these supplements (about 7,500 milligrams of citrate for every 1,000 milligrams of calcium) leads to urinary excretion of some of the citrate. The citrate ion helps keep calcium in the urine in solution, so that stones are less likely to form or grow. But if you don't have a tendency to form stones in the first place, then this advantage is irrelevant.

There's another feature of supplements that is probably more important than relative absorbability. That is pharmaceutical formulation. There is a science to formulating a tablet that will not break up in the bottle during shipment, but will still disintegrate in the stomach so that your digestive system has a chance to absorb it. A tablet so hard that it goes through you like a bullet will do you no good. Here is where the supplements differ from one another most profoundly. The following table shows the results of published studies of two critical factors for calcium supplements—time for a tablet to disintegrate when placed in liquid, and percent dissolved in thirty minutes when placed in an acid solution similar to gastric juice. You want short disintegration times and high solubility in a supplement. Here the chemical nature of salt makes no difference. As you can readily see, some oyster shell preparations are at the top of the list, some at the bottom. It is all a matter of the care and skill with which the manufacturer compounds the tablet.

Unfortunately for the consumer, existing regulations do not require supplement manufacturers to disclose how well their products disintegrate and dissolve. So you can't tell for sure. One thing you can do, however, is to do your own testing. Take a tablet from a supplement you'd like to con-

DISINTEGRATION AND DISSOLVING TIMES
OF CALCIUM SUPPLEMENTS

	Disintegration time (minutes)	% dissolved at 30 minutes
Os-Cal 500 (Marion)	8.8	88
Caltrate 600 (Lederle)	1.0	69
Supplical (Warner-Lambert)	*	98
Posture (Ayerst)	1.0	56
Tums (Norcliff Thayer)	*	100
Oyster Shell Calcium (Nature Made)	under 1.0	100
Bio-Cal (Miles)	30	5
Potent Calcium (Gen'l Nutr. Corp.)	over 60	5
Your Life Calcium (Your Life)	over 60	6
Nature's Wonder (Ford Lab)	over 60	7
Oyster Shell Calcium (Foods Plus)	over 60	9
Oyster Shell Calcium (Caldor)	over 60	8

* Chewable tablet—therefore disintegrated before swallowing.

sider and drop it in a glass of warm water. Swirl it gently every now and then. If it's not completely disintegrated in one hour, you have reason to wonder whether it would do much better in your stomach. Carbonate and phosphate preparations will not dissolve under these conditions, but they should disintegrate, leaving you with a uniform milky suspension.

There are reasons to choose *against* certain kinds of supplements. Dolomite is one to avoid. Dolomite is a complex mineral containing calcium and magnesium carbonates. It is a natural mineral, and, like most such, it contains traces of many other substances, laid down with the calcium and magnesium at the time the mineral was formed aeons ago. These substances include cadmium, uranium, mercury, arsenic, and lead. The quantities of these poisonous materials are generally small, but if you were to take dolomite regularly, particularly in large doses (more than one to two tablets daily), you could perhaps build up toxic levels of these other elements.

Dolomite has been marketed as "natural," as if somehow that meant that it was better or more healthful than other sources. That, of course, is nonsense. There is no scientific evidence to support such a claim, and there are mountains of evidence concerning the toxicity of the other elements it contains. Dolomite is natural, all right, and so are the poisons it contains. Also, a mineral such as dolomite is seen as attractive by many people, both because it contains magnesium—and some people are concerned about getting enough magnesium every day—and because it is a "natural" mineral, as if "natural" were somehow better than "pure" or "safe."

Another supplement to avoid is bonemeal. Bonemeal consists of ground, processed animal bone. Since bonemeal contains all of the minerals of bone, in exactly the right balance, you might think it would be the ideal supplement. And it might be, if it were prepared from the bones of the young beef cattle slaughtered by the thousands in the Midwestern United States every day. But some batches of bonemeal have been found to contain substantial quantities of lead, and, as with dolomite, regular use of this supplement could produce lead poisoning.

The contaminated batches of bonemeal were found to have been prepared from old horses which had grazed for years beside busy highways. Lead from automobile emissions had been taken up by the grass and plants, eaten by the horses, and deposited in their bones. In fact, lead—and many other heavy metal pollutants, such as plutonium, radium, and strontium—become concentrated in bone through normal physiologic processes. So eating the bones of old grazing animals is not safe, at least if the animals have spent their lives in a polluted environment. That's why we said that bones of *young* beef cattle would be a better source.

One might wonder how these potentially harmful preparations are allowed to be sold to the American public, and even more, why they are promoted as healthful. To begin with, the regulations governing nutritional supplements are much less stringent than those governing drugs. Packagers of products such as dolomite and bonemeal are not required by the FDA to analyze their preparations for traces of toxic elements, much less to print on their labels the results of such analyses. So long as these products aren't accompanied by therapeutic claims, they are not regulated as drugs. Bonemeal, as we have seen, would be a good supplement if its manufacturers took pains to control the purity of the bones from which they made their product.

As a matter of fact, we would have been inclined to recommend bonemeal and equivalent products as an attractive supplement—that is, if you must take a supplement at all—but we cannot do so until we can be assured of a product free of contamination by environmental lead. So we recommend that you look for evidence of purity on the label, that is, a statement that the product has been analyzed and has been found to contain no lead, or at least that its content of toxic elements is below levels considered safe by the Environmental Protection Agency (EPA).

How, then, should you select a supplement? Until we have firm information about the relative safety or ill effects of the negative ions accompanying calcium in these supplements, we cannot really choose among them on the basis of their chemical form. A calcium phosphate preparation does seem to have an advantage for some persons because it contains phosphorus, the other essential bulk mineral in bone. But there still is no evidence to support a claim that calcium phosphate works better. So we suggest only a few simple rules:

1. Choose a form that gives you the most calcium in the smallest number of pills; you're less likely to forget to take your entire day's dosage that way.
2. Choose a form that gives you the most calcium for the dollar.
3. Choose a good manufacturer. Whenever a new market opens up—such as the one the "calcium craze" has created—a lot of fast-buck operators move in to exploit the public interest. Reputable pharmaceutical manufacturers can be exploitative too, but they're more likely to follow good manufacturing practices. Not only purity and uniformity are at stake here. There is the matter of whether the tablet will break up in the stomach and dissolve.

Taking calcium supplements may be necessary for some people. The reason is simply that they can't get as much calcium as they need from their diet, because: (1) they have health problems that preclude their eating dairy products in the amount necessary to meet their requirement for calcium; (2) they don't like dairy products or other foods rich in calcium, and realistically are unlikely to make the needed dietary changes; or (3) they eat so little that it is hard to get enough calcium, regardless of what they do eat. We noted that this last reason usually implies physi al inactivity, and, if so, that it was likely that calcium deficiency wasn't their only problem, and thus getting more calcium might not help. But for the first two reasons, maybe a calcium supplement would be beneficial. Even so, there would still be the problems of cost, forgetting to take the pills, and the other drawbacks of supplements.

EXPLOITATION

We want to point an accusing finger at the exploitation of women's fears in calcium advertising. Much of the advertising for calcium supplements creates a foundation of fear and then builds upon it. Such an approach calls women's attention to a problem they didn't really know existed; it exaggerates how common the problem is. Then it promises prevention: just buy this product, or take this test, or else . . .

The graphic depiction of deformity is not an ethical way to sell calcium supplements. We take particular note of the use of young and old look-alikes in this advertising. The older of the pair is deformed by what passes for osteoporosis, and there is the clear implication that the use of the advertised product will prevent this ugly transformation. One might contrast this approach with that used by the dairy industry over the years. Its advertisements have consistently shown healthy, vigorous, active people in association with its products. We feel, in short, that advertisers can take the high road or the low, and that there has been a good deal of traffic on the latter.

28

Making Good Things Better: Fortification of Foods with Calcium

Fortification of various natural foods with calcium has been occurring with increasing frequency in the past two or three years. By and large, we think this is a good move. It is better

*to get calcium in fortified foods than in supplement pills.
Fortified foods can help us get the calcium we need without
having to remember to take pills—and in the long run less
expensively, too.*

There is an alternative to supplements that we consider
preferable—fortification of foods. Calcium preparations can
be added during the manufacture or processing of some of
the foods we buy and eat. In this way we get more calcium
without having to remember to take pills, without paying the
extra cost of a pill, and without even thinking about what we
are doing.

The general decrease in energy expenditure in our society
over the last fifty years has resulted in an across-the-board
decline in food intake. That's been necessary in order to
avoid a national epidemic of obesity. But with less total food
intake, we get less of certain key nutrients, such as calcium
and iron. Our society recognized the need to fortify the food
chain in the case of iron as far back as 1942. With decreased
total food intake, we had reached the point where many
women, during their reproductive years, could not get
enough iron in an ordinary diet to compensate for monthly
menstrual losses and childbearing. And so, by federal law—
and by state law in more than forty states—we now add iron
to white bread flour. Even earlier, we added iodine to salt to
assure a high enough iodine intake to permit normal thyroid
function. There are several other examples. For instance, we
add vitamins A and D to milk (vitamin A must be added, by
law, to reduced-fat milk; the addition of vitamin D is voluntary). And white bread flour has not only added iron, but
additional quantities of other essential nutrients. Even fluoridation of municipal water supplies is an example of fortification. Should calcium be next?

There are three ways our nation can approach this issue.
One would be to select certain foods and specify by law that
they must contain a certain level of calcium (like iron fortification of white bread). Another would be the modification of

existing laws and regulations that unintentionally result in a food's containing less calcium than it might. And the third is the voluntary introduction of calcium-fortified foods into the market by food manufacturers and processors.

It is not likely that we will see mandatory fortification very soon. Rethinking and revising existing composition standards seems feasible, however, though it may be difficult. For example, we could revise milk standards. (One might have thought that milk was "standard" already, but in fact each state has regulations that define the content of solids and fat in any product marketed as milk. This is a protection against unscrupulous bottlers who might water down the product that the cow gives us.)

Fifteen years or so ago, California raised its milk standards. Although the focus was on solids, not calcium, the result was that milk sold in California contained, in some cases, 20 percent more calcium than milk sold in other states. Similar milk standards laws have been introduced recently in many states, and some states have already adopted them. But it is a slow process. The opposition to this seemingly reasonable legislation comes from two sources: (1) fear that the extra cost of the higher solids content would hurt sales (it didn't in California); and (2) the resistance of the milk processors, who would have to adhere to tougher processing standards. On balance, upward revision of milk standards is a good move. It's not a total solution to the calcium intake problem, but it is one small step. (In fact, there won't be a single action we can take that will solve the whole problem. The solution will consist of many small steps.)

Another step would be to take a second look at regulations governing the presence of bone particles in processed meats. Increasingly, the meats we eat, particularly in restaurants, from fast food outlets, on airplanes, and so forth, have been extensively processed to remove bone and other undesirable components. (In fact, nearly half the meat consumed in this country is mechanically "processed".) Sometimes mechanical deboning equipment, cutting as close to the bone as possible to reduce waste, leaves tiny bone particles in the meat product. To control this, USDA regulations govern the precise quantity and size of bone particles such meats can contain. Those regulations are vigorously defended by two groups: butchers, whose jobs are being lost to mechanical deboners, and consumer advocates, who interpret the presence of bone particles as evidence of corporate greed. The pressures of both groups have tended to increase the cost of processed meat products, for they have pushed the acceptable level of particle down to a microscopic level. We think, also, that they may make the product less nutritious. For bone, as we have seen, can be an excellent source of calcium.

Now, we certainly are not advocating the introduction of big chunks of bone into our foods. Bone slivers could well be unsafe; they certainly would be aesthetically displeasing; and they probably wouldn't be nutritionally very helpful anyway, for we don't have a digestive system like an alligator's. If the calcium in bone is to be accessible to us, the bone particles will probably need to be the size of powder. That's why these regulations need to be looked at anew, to see whether someone's good intentions haven't in fact resulted in the unnecessary loss of a nutritional benefit. If so, perhaps they can be modified. Once again, just one small step.

The third approach seems to offer the most immediate opportunity, both for the consumer and for the food industry—the voluntary addition of suitable calcium preparations to various foods. We believe that this will be seen as such an attractive marketing opportunity by food processors that we will soon see an explosion of calcium-fortified foods on grocery store shelves. A few products to which extra calcium has been added are being aggressively promoted, precisely on the basis of their newly enhanced calcium content. So read the labels. (Incidentally, one result of this food fortification is that the tables on the calcium content of foods will have to be revised.)

Here are a few of the fortified products, just to give some idea both of the variety of ways calcium fortification can be accomplished, and of the ingenuity of American food processors.

Both General Mills and Pillsbury now add calcium sulfate to their all-purpose flours. One result is that two chocolate chip cookies now contain 17 milligrams of calcium, instead of 2.5 milligrams. Not a big change, but a step in the right direction. On the other end of the scale is a breakfast cereal called Dairy Crisp, marketed by Pet Foods. This product is fortified with whey *and* calcium phosphate to such a high level that one bowl, with four ounces of milk, provides 1,000 milligrams of calcium in one serving. Yet another type of preparation is a product called Calci-milk, which takes care of two problems at once. It is lactose-reduced (for those persons with lactose intolerance) and it has added calcium to boot. So a single eight-ounce glass provides 500 milligrams of calcium. That's about 50–60 percent more than most standard milks. Bakers are now authorized to market a product they can label as "enriched special formula bread." One slice contains 38 milligrams of calcium, slightly more than other breads. At least one baker, the maker of Hollywood Special Formula Bread, has added enough calcium sulfate to raise the calcium content per slice to about 120 milligrams, three to five times the content of ordinary bread. Soft drink and beverage manufacturers have been swift to move into the fortified products market. The Coca-Cola Company has test marketed a new Tab containing 100 milligrams of calcium (as calcium chloride) per twelve-ounce can. Citrus Hill orange and grapefruit juices are now available with sufficient added calcium to make a glass of juice equivalent to a glass of milk. This may, in fact, be an effective way of increasing the calcium consumption of teenage girls. If they won't drink milk (which would be preferable), at least they can get calcium in fortified juices and soft drinks.

The calcium sources that food fortifiers might use are similar to, but not quite the same as, the supplements. One of the oldest additives is calcium carbonate. The British used it to fortify wheat flour in World War II, to assure an adequate calcium supply for growing children when much of the dairy output of Great Britain was being diverted to military use. We did the same thing in this country briefly, but dropped the practice some years ago. At least one Canadian meat packer is now adding calcium carbonate to certain of its processed meats.

Perhaps a better source for many purposes is nonfat dry milk powder. It is a very good additive to bread, both improving the texture and enriching the nutrient content in many ways besides the added calcium. Nonfat dry milk costs more than calcium carbonate—and so is used less often—but it provides other nutrients in addition to calcium. So it's still a bargain. Moreover, it would seem to be good for the economy of the country, putting to good use a part of the U.S. surplus dairy production.

Another good source of calcium for food fortification is whey. Whey is the vitamin- and mineral-rich liquid that is a by-product of certain types of cheese manufacture (notably cottage cheese). Most of the protein stays behind as the curd, and the liquid whey carries most of the mineral. Whey can be freeze-dried and added to a variety of products. Dairy Crisp cereal, for example, is fortified with whey concentrates and calcium phosphate. At least one new company (IGENE, Inc. of Columbia, Maryland) specializes in the production of freeze-dried whey concentrates for sale to food processors and manufacturers. They produce a product called "La Cal" that contains 950 milligrams of calcium per tablespoon! This is too concentrated for safe home use, but could be very attractive to bakers and other food processors. At least one East Coast dairy adds this product to its cottage cheese. Like Miss Muffet, it combines the curds with the whey. This combination converts cottage cheese from a mediocre to an excellent source of calcium. And since it contains few calories, this kind of fortified cottage cheese retains its image as a diet food.

Yet another good natural source of calcium for certain types of food would be bonemeal. Small amounts of pure bonemeal (free of lead and other environmental contaminants we discussed in Chapter 27) added to sausages, luncheon meats, frankfurters, chili, stews, spaghetti sauces, and similar meats and meat products would greatly enrich their nutritional value. Bonemeal could do for meats what bones do for sardines. Further, protein intake increases our requirement for calcium. If we are going to be a nation of heavy meat eaters, it makes sense to see to it that at least some of our meats provide some calcium.

The mineral in bonemeal is, obviously, calcium phosphate. Pure chemical forms of calcium phosphate could just as well be used instead, and in fact Dairy Crisp uses calcium phosphate in addition to whey concentrates. Other refined chemical forms of calcium are also used. For example, the source of the extra calcium in all-purpose flour and in Hollywood Special Formula Bread is calcium sulfate, and the calcium in Tab is calcium chloride.

Food chemistry is a complicated field. However, it should be clear that many different forms of calcium have been and can be used. Given the surge of interest in increasing calcium intake, we will soon encounter other forms of calcium in food products as well.

Food fortification raises the same public policy questions as does setting a recommended allowance for various nutrients. Just as not everybody *needs* as much as the allowance—but some do—so not everybody will *need* the extra calcium in a fortified food or beverage. Some, and perhaps many, will. But this is true for all nutrient fortifications. People living by the ocean and eating a lot of seafood do not need iodine added to their salt. Men do not need the extra iron in white bread. In the same way, a teenage boy drinking over two quarts of milk a day doesn't need a calcium-fortified breakfast cereal. That's why questions of safety become important whenever we consider fortification with any essential nutrient. The goal, at a policy level, is to come up with standards that do the most good for the most people, without exposing others to unacceptable risks. It is not an easy task to accomplish. The extra iron doesn't hurt the men who eat white bread and the extra iodine doesn't hurt coastal dwellers. We need to be certain that the extra calcium doesn't hurt those who don't need it. For that reason, we favor relatively lower levels of fortification in a large number of foodstuffs, instead of higher levels in a few foods. If some foods are fortified to very high levels, it may become possible to overdose on calcium from food, just like supplements. A breakfast cereal that provides 1,000 milligrams of calcium in a single serving could well be an example of too much of a good thing.

Another advantage to opting for low levels of fortification in a large number of foods is that we're more likely to get the other nutrients we need for calcium utilization and bone health. Variety is still a mainstay of good nutrition.

In general we are enthusiastic about fortification, particularly the voluntary, food-by-food, brand-by-brand type. People who don't need extra calcium aren't forced to get it if they don't want to. And this approach is likely to increase average calcium intake sooner than any change dependent upon enacting new laws or regulations.

WHAT YOU SHOULD
DO—OSTEOPOROSIS

29

Are You at Risk for Osteoporosis?

Small-boned, light-skinned, thin, blue-eyed, fair-haired, sedentary women are at higher risk of osteoporosis than are bigger-boned, overweight, or hard-working women. There is no one cause of all cases of osteoporosis. Various combinations of causes are probably responsible for most cases, with different people having different combinations. Several factors are known to be part of the picture: inadequate calcium intake, the loss of female hormones at menopause, inadequate physical exercise, alcohol abuse, smoking, and heredity. And there are probably other factors still unknown.

Are you at risk for developing osteoporosis? Certain marks, or characteristics, or life-style factors—what we call risk factors—allow us to say, "This group of women is likely to get osteoporosis and that group of women is unlikely to develop osteoporosis." But although we can describe *groups* in which the chances are high or low, for individuals, prediction cannot really be made with certainty. Some women who seem to be in a low-risk group will go on to develop osteoporotic fracture, and some who seem to be in a high-risk group will not. But these will be exceptions. However, while our ability to make predictions is limited, it is still helpful to know which risk factors you have.

There is something else you need to know about risk factors: There is no absolutely safe level for most of them. As your level of exposure goes up, so too does your risk. At low levels of exposure your risk may be so small that you can safely forget about it. Virtually everything we do in life carries with it some risk. It is not our purpose to scare you. Rather, it is to tell you what factors may be increasing or decreasing your risk for osteoporosis—so that you can take control of your own situation and change those factors that may be increasing your risk.

There are hereditary and constitutional risk factors, lifestyle risk factors, and medical risk factors. Each of these risk factors has a more or less firmly established association—which scientists believe is cause and effect—with osteoporosis.

First, the hereditary or constitutional factors. Women with older female relatives on either side of the family who have developed osteoporotic fractures may have inherited some of the same predisposing features that led to osteoporosis in their relatives. Of course, this doesn't mean that a person is certain to develop osteoporosis. But if we put all the women whose older female relatives had osteoporosis into one group and all the women whose older female relatives did not have osteoporosis into another group, and followed both groups for thirty or forty years, there would be more cases of osteoporosis in the first group than in the second. Nobody yet knows precisely how many more.

In much the same way, women who are small, who have never weighed more than 130 pounds in their lives, who are thin, fair-complexioned, light-haired, or blue-eyed, or who have scant body hair all seem to be at greater risk than, for example, larger, darker caucasian women. It is not surprising, therefore, that those who are distinctly overweight have less risk of osteoporosis. In fact, their risk is only about one third that of women generally. (This is probably the first positive thing you have ever heard about being overweight!) After menopause, women continue to produce small quantities of female hormones; some scientists suggest that heavy women are at lower risk for osteoporosis because they produce more female hormones after menopause than thin women do. Other scientists note that heavy women have more muscle as well as the extra fat, and others point to the extra physical work of carrying around those surplus pounds. Nobody knows for sure.

Pregnancy and lactation are other constitutional factors that influence the risk of osteoporosis. Some people assume that pregnancy increases the risk of osteoporosis. However, the more children women in First World countries have, the less their risk for future osteoporotic fracture. Several studies have shown this quite clearly. The same seems to be true for breast feeding, though here the evidence is more scant. The protection is not great, but it does appear to be real.

Next, the life-style factors. Most important is physical activity—exercise, or work—built right into the fabric of our everyday lives. The more the better. Women who are inactive are at substantially greater risk than women who work hard physically. There was a time when it was considered inappropriate not just for women to engage in sports, but even to do physical work. Women of means hired others to do their manual labor. And so, in a certain sense, it was quite ladylike to get osteoporosis.

Diet is another life-style factor. As we have already seen, diets low in calcium are insufficient to meet our daily requirements, and diets high in protein or salt create a higher calcium requirement, often higher than a woman's actual calcium intake. If you know that your calcium intake is low, or your protein and sodium intakes are high—or both—then know that you are at higher risk.

Cigarettes, alcohol, and caffeine are also definitely osteoporosis risk factors. Cigarette smoking increases a person's risk of osteoporosis leading to fracture by about 50 percent. The bone density of women who smoke is lower than that of those who do not, and menopause in smokers occurs one or two years earlier. It is also suspected that smokers may break down estrogen more rapidly than do nonsmokers, so they have lower estrogen levels generally. Smoking has been implicated in a lengthening litany of health problems: aggravation of allergies, injuries due to burns, chronic bronchitis, emphysema, hypertension (high blood pressure), coronary artery disease, stroke, peptic ulcer, miscarriage, prematurity, low birth weight, stillbirths, cancers (of the lung, esophagus, larynx, stomach, bowel, urinary bladder, and breast), and on and on. Smoking holds so many dangers, and their implications are so serious, that no one who smokes for several years can expect to escape without penalty. Smoking is a threat particularly to the health of women.

Alcohol abuse is even worse than smoking from the standpoint of bone health. No one knows exactly how much worse, because alcoholics have many health problems, and osteoporosis is generally not the worst of them. Nevertheless, studies have shown that the bone mass of a typical alcohol abuser has been reduced to a level one would expect to find in a person of the same sex forty years older! High blood levels of alcohol poison the living cells of many of our tissues, certainly the liver and brain and, we have every reason to believe, bone as well. There is a fine line between an acceptable alcohol intake and too much. So far as we know, moderate drinking does not harm the bones. But more than three drinks a day is probably too much from the standpoint of bone health. There are probably many secret alcohol abusers among middle-aged women. Only you know whether this is a risk factor for you. If it is, it *cannot* be offset by taking more calcium. You must cut down your alcohol intake, or cut it out entirely.

Caffeine, whether taken as coffee, tea, or cola beverages, leads to increased loss of calcium both through the kidneys and the intestine. The effect, however, is small, and if your daily coffee intake is no more than two or three cups, the calcium loss can be offset with a few swallows of milk. But if you're a heavy coffee drinker—say, ten to twenty cups a day —then your caffeine consumption is an important risk factor for osteoporosis.

Major Sources of Caffeine
(and their content in milligrams per serving)

Brewed coffee	160–250
Instant coffee	50–75
Brewed tea	30–70
Instant tea	30–40
Colas	35–50

There are other, smaller food sources of caffeine or caffeinelike substances, such as chocolate. But taken all together, it is unlikely that they would contribute more caffeine than that in a single cup of coffee. As we have said, there is no magic number of milligrams at which the risk factor begins. Think of this as a continuum.

Finally, the medical factors. Most important is the use of steroid hormones, called "glucocorticoids," "corticosteroids," or just "steroids." These drugs are sometimes used as a last resort to treat certain diseases of the lungs or the connective tissues, where they may produce blessed relief but often with serious side effects. These drugs, in the doses necessary to produce their desired effects, lead to the breakdown of many body tissues—skin, muscle, and bone. In patients with long-term treatment on corticosteroids, the chance of incurring osteoporotic fractures is about ten times higher than average. There is basically nothing medicine can now do to reduce this risk, though efforts are under way both to find safe treatments for the diseases in which these drugs are used and to protect the bones when steroids do have to be used.

Therapy with thyroid hormone for thyroid deficiency is also associated with an increased risk for osteoporosis. Thyroid hormone is exceedingly important, and definitely ought to be used in patients who have true thyroid deficiencies. But it is important for physicians to get the dose right, because too much thyroid hormone seems to increase the risk of osteoporosis. The same is true for hyperthyroidism, in which the patient's thyroid is overactive.

People who have had their stomachs removed—generally

because of ulcers—are also known to be at higher risk for osteoporosis. This has been attributed to problems with absorption of calcium and vitamin D. However, recently another explanation, with implications for many more patients, has come to light. Antacids based on aluminum compounds have long been one of the mainstays in the treatment of gastric hyperacidity, indigestion, "heartburn," and peptic ulcer disease. Unfortunately, one of the effects of this type of antacid is an increased loss of calcium in the urine. (This happens because the aluminum in the antacid binds phosphorus in the intestine and thereby prevents its absorption. Often that leads to a fall in the level of phosphorus in the body fluids. When phosphorus levels in the extracellular fluid are high, then urine calcium excretion falls, and when phosphorus levels in the extracellular fluid fall, urine calcium rises.)

Only recently have we recognized the calcium-wasting effect of the aluminum-containing antacids. It helps explain the problem of osteoporosis in persons who have had gastrectomies because, as a rule, the stomach is removed only after years of more or less unsuccessful antacid therapy. So by the time a person's stomach has been taken out, there may well have been years of unrecognized loss of calcium in the urine and consequent bone damage. People need to be aware of this problem. For even without a gastrectomy, long-term use of aluminum-containing antacids can cause permanent bone damage. However, such problems are not inevitable. To offset the effect of these antacids, we need only increase the calcium intake. One way to do so—a way that kills two birds with one stone—is to use milk as an antacid. It supplies calcium and itself functions as a good antacid. Or calcium carbonate can be used. It works as an antacid (look at the success of Tums!), and it also supplies calcium. So there is more than one option here.

Another example of how treatment of medical conditions can alter the risk of osteoporosis is the treatment of patients with kidney stones. As we explained earlier, kidney stones may develop for several different reasons. Whatever the cause, most stones contain calcium. Physicians usually place patients with kidney stones on low-calcium diets, even though dietary calcium is a significant contributory factor in only a small fraction of all kidney stone cases. At one time, it was generally believed that adults didn't need much calcium, so physicians reasoned that restricting calcium in people with kidney stones couldn't hurt, and might help. We now know that calcium *is* important for adults, especially adult women. Physicians need to be very cautious about placing any woman on a low-calcium diet. They need to be certain that calcium intake is really part of the problem.

Finally, there is another medical condition that signals an altered risk of developing osteoporosis. This is a form of arthritis which generally comes on in old age and is often termed "hypertrophic osteoarthritis." One of its manifestations is the presence of small, hard bumps at the sides of the last joint of the fingers. Curiously, people who get this problem seem only rarely to get osteoporosis. So if you have this kind of arthritis, or if it runs in your female relatives, the chances are you are at less than average risk for osteoporosis.

Some risk factors are no doubt a lot more important than others. Long-term alcohol abuse or long-term treatment with glucocorticoids (such as prednisone or other cortisonelike drugs) taken internally almost certainly lead to bone damage.

It is useful to think about risk factors in terms of how they pile up. For example, low dietary calcium, low levels of physical activity, cigarette smoking, high caffeine consumption, and high alcohol consumption often occur together in the same woman. And together they spell trouble. But all the items on this list are life-style factors, factors *you* can change. In fact, many of the risk factors associated with osteoporosis depend upon personal habits and individual choices. Some risk factors, like heredity, you can't change. These should warn you to take especially seriously the ones you can change.

RISK FACTORS FOR OSTEOPOROSIS

Increased Risk	*Decreased Risk*

HEREDITARY AND CONSTITUTIONAL

Family history of osteoporosis	Obesity
	Many children
Small size, fair skin, blue eyes	
Few or no children	

LIFE-STYLE

Low calcium intake	Adequate calcium intake
Inactivity	Hard physical work,
Alcohol abuse	regular exercise
Cigarette smoking	
High protein intake	
High sodium intake	
High caffeine intake	

HEALTH INFLUENCES

Corticosteroid treatment	Hypertrophic
Excess thyroid hormone	osteoarthritis
Use of aluminum-containing antacids, gastrectomy	Estrogen replacement therapy
Restricted mobility	
Calcium restriction for kidney stones	
Early menopause	

30
Bone Scanning

Bone scanning, a research technique, provides surprisingly little useful information when applied to individuals. The site most often measured in bone scanning clinics, the wrist, does not reflect bone status in other parts of the body very accurately. The bone-scanning technique has been seriously oversold.

Recently bone-scanning clinics have proliferated, many set up as for-profit franchises, others promoted by hospitals. Their advertising approach is similar to that used in promoting calcium supplements. (Some clinics even sell the supplements!) Their approach builds upon the fears of women, just as does the advertising for calcium pills. "Don't *you* become a victim of this 'silent epidemic.' Get your bone status tested in our center, and we will tell you what lies ahead for you."

Not only is this exploitative, but the results of such bone scanning don't really tell you anything. Most bone scanners use an instrument that determines bone density at the wrist. The use of this site has been justly criticized by scientists working in the field, because bone density at the wrist is not a good reflection of bone density in the key parts of the body, the spine and hip, for example.

And this is not the only problem. The client is led to believe that a second, follow-up measurement of bone mass can reveal how rapidly she is losing bone. Even many physicians think that. But the facts are that existing methods are not sensitive enough to pick up the kinds of changes even a woman suffering rapid bone loss is likely to exhibit. Even using a more relevant anatomical site like the spine and the best equipment available today, two or more measurements of bone mass on the same individual—even on the same day —do not give exactly the same results, and thus differences obtained in measurements separated by a period of months do not necessarily reflect change. In fact, an amount of bone loss over a year that would be of real concern can easily be missed (a false-negative result) or can be indicated by mistake (a false-positive result). Using current methods, false-negative results will occur in perhaps half of all women who are undergoing serious bone loss, and false positive results in about half of all women who have no problem whatsoever. A flip of a coin could tell you about as much.

Simply put, the bone-scanning technique has been seriously oversold, and stands to do much mischief in the years ahead. A single measurement of bone mass in an individual woman yields a surprisingly limited amount of useful information. Probably the best that can be done is tentatively to place that woman within the lower, middle, or upper one third of women by bone mass. That, unfortunately, doesn't tell us very much about the future risk of fracture. The measurement of bone mass by current bone-scanning techniques is an extremely valuable research tool when averaged over a large group of women. However, these methods cannot help individual women make decisions.

Should you pay $150–250 to have your bones scanned? We think that, for most women, the answer is no. Chances are you won't be told to do anything different as a result of the evaluation than you should have done anyhow. But if an expensive computer printout and high-tech equipment increase your motivation to follow the commonsense advice in this book, then maybe it is worth your investment.

31
The Estrogen Question

To take or not to take estrogen after menopause is a personal choice, but one that can be based upon facts and individual needs as well as preferences. Estrogen replacement therapy (ERT) controls the symptoms of menopause and reduces the likelihood of developing osteoporotic fractures and coronary heart disease. However, ERT increases the risk of gallbladder disease and uterine cancer, results in continued menstruation, and requires medical supervision.

Even when the topic of our talk has been calcium we are almost always asked by someone in the audience, "Should I take estrogen?" It is an important question, and obviously a lot of women are looking for an answer.

Probably the word "should" gets us off on the wrong foot altogether. No woman ought to feel that there is one best answer for everyone, or that she is obligated to do one thing or the other. There are so many pros and cons that the choice has to be a personal one. Some aspects of estrogen replacement therapy (ERT) will be important for one woman but unimportant for another. And so one answer will be right for the first woman, but wrong for the second.

Only you can make your own choice about ERT. What we shall do in this chapter is list for you the principal advantages and disadvantages of ERT, and then explain them. Then your decision can be well informed.

ADVANTAGES:

- ERT, starting at menopause and continuing for at least five to ten years, reduces the risk of osteoporotic fracture by at least 50–60 percent, maybe more.

- ERT reduces the risk of coronary heart disease by at least 50 percent.

- ERT reduces or eliminates hot flashes.

- ERT prevents atrophy (dryness and irritation) of vulvar and vaginal tissues.

- ERT prevents other discomforts of menopause that some women experience, such as nervousness and irritability.

DISADVANTAGES:

- ERT generally results in continued menstruation (though it does not prolong fertility).

- ERT requires medical supervision and is a part of what some have called the "medicalization" of the menopause: a normal part of a woman's life is handled as though it were a disease.

- ERT increases the risk of developing cancer of the lining of the uterus. Experts disagree about how much the risk increases, but it probably at least doubles.

- ERT increases the risk of gallbladder disease, probably by about 50 percent.

- ERT *may* increase very slightly the risk of breast cancer. The size of the increase, if any, is unknown. Most studies have found no increase at all. If there is any increase in risk, it is probably no greater than 10 percent.

- If you still have a uterus, most physicians will prescribe progesteronelike compounds (progestogens) along with the estrogen. These eliminate the risk of cancer of the uterus entirely, but they have certain disadvantages. For some women they contribute to premenstrual syndrome (or PMS), and many of the most commonly prescribed progestogens counteract some of the beneficial effects of ERT on coronary heart disease. So what a woman gains in protection from cancer she may more than lose in terms of heart attack risk.

These are the facts. But knowing them can sometimes be as confusing as not knowing. It is hard to add them up and feel sure you have the right answer. How, for example, do you compare an increased risk of getting cancer of the uterus and a decreased risk of coronary heart disease?

We can help you evaluate some of these trade-offs—at least the more readily measurable risks and benefits—by examining with you some data taken from the best scientific study of this matter that has been published to date. The following figures provide estimates of how many deaths would be both saved and caused by ERT in women aged fifty to seventy-five.

Here "relative risk" is a quantitative way to approach some of the advantages and disadvantages of ERT. A relative risk of 1.0 means that ERT makes no difference in your risk of succumbing to the disorder in question. A relative risk of 0.5 means that ERT cuts the risk in half. One of 2.0 means the risk is doubled. The mortality figures are expressed as deaths per 100,000 women. (This is because risk factors like these are valid only when averaged over very large numbers of people.) The positive figures (such as +187) represent extra deaths *caused* by ERT, and the negative figures (such as −563) represent deaths *prevented*.

For osteoporosis, ERT can be expected to save about 563

Condition	Relative Risk	Change in Mortality per 100,000
Osteoporotic fractures	0.4	− 563
Gallbladder disease	1.5	+ 2
Uterine cancer	2.0	+ 63
Breast cancer	1.1	+ 187
Coronary heart disease	0.5	− 5,250
Net change		− 5,561

lives per 100,000 women—lives that would otherwise be cut short because of complications of hip fractures caused by osteoporosis. But offsetting that gain would be 252 lives lost because of gallbladder disease, cancer of the lining of the uterus, and cancer of the breast, combined. In each instance the calculation takes into consideration the natural risk a woman would have of succumbing to the disease without ERT. That is partly why the 10 percent increase in breast cancer risk (relative risk of 1.1) is expected to produce more deaths than a 100 percent increase in uterine cancer risk (relative risk of 2.0). (It is not, in fact, known that ERT increases breast cancer risk at all, but most experts, in doing these kinds of calculations, will factor in a small increase of this sort just to be certain that they are erring on the side of safety.) Breast cancer is expected to cause greater loss of life both because it is more common to start with, and because it is not as easy to cure as cancer of the uterus is. Nevertheless, taken together, the benefit from prevention of osteoporosis still outweighs the loss due to cancer.

But more surprising than all of these changes is the effect of ERT on deaths related to heart attacks. It dwarfs all of the other effects. Strangely enough, most physicians don't talk to their menopausal patients about this benefit. We say "strangely" because there is no great mystery about this protection against heart disease. We have known about it for years. It just hasn't been integrated into this issue of ERT. How many times have you heard of a woman in her thirties or forties keeling over from a heart attack? Almost never. It is something that happens to men. Women do get heart attacks, of course, but they are very rare before menopause, for the simple reason that the female hormone causes cholesterol and fat in the blood to be packaged in what has been called a "safe" pattern. Male hormones (and the absence of female hormones) reverse that pattern and make it "unsafe." So women are relatively protected from problems of atherosclerosis and coronary heart disease, and that protection lasts as long as the body has female hormones. (Here it makes essentially no difference whether those hormones are from the woman's ovaries or from ERT.)

But there is more. The previous table presents figures for ERT without the progestogens that most physicians now prescribe to prevent the development of cancer of the uterus. The table that follows refigures the estimated risks of ERT, but now in combination with progestogens (sometimes called HRT—hormone replacement therapy). The progestogens offer some protection against cancer of the uterus, and for the sake of argument we have assumed that they also protect against the small increase in risk estimated for breast cancer. Note that the relative risks for uterine and breast cancers drop to 1.0. But we have also had to factor in a reduction of some of estrogen's benefits on coronary heart disease: To be conservative, we have kept most of the protection of ERT, letting the relative risk of coronary heart disease rise only a little, from 0.5 to 0.6. (Actually, it may rise even more than that.) Even with these conservative figures, look what happens in terms of overall deaths.

Condition	Relative Risk	Change in Mortality per 100,000
Osteoporotic fractures	0.4	− 563
Gallbladder disease	1.5	+ 2
Uterine cancer	1.0	0
Breast cancer	1.0	0
Coronary heart disease	0.6	− 4,200
Net change		− 4,761

Compare these numbers with the previous ones. Lives are still being saved—but not nearly as many as before. Yes, we wiped out the increase in cancer deaths with progestogens, and we have breathed a sigh of relief over that! But we have lost far more than we have gained because of the reduced protection against heart disease.

Many choices in medicine are like this one. You gain something, but you lose something different. It does no good to pretend otherwise. And these are just the quantifiable issues. This kind of calculation cannot evaluate the annoyance of continuing menstrual periods and of ongoing PMS, the annual medical checkups and periodic uterine biopsies, the worry and anxiety that surround episodes of irregular bleeding while on ERT, and the like. For some women these quality-of-life issues may be far more important than for others, and so the decision for them may be different.

There is another point that doesn't often get talked about. A surprisingly large fraction of women have had their uterus removed by the time they reach the age of menopause. Figures vary from one part of the country to the other, but the number is probably between 35 and 45 percent, or roughly two out of every five women. For them, there can be no fear of getting cancer of the lining of the uterus—for of course they no longer have one. And yet we often encounter women who have had a hysterectomy and who are worried about taking ERT because they have heard that it causes cancer. This is one problem they are spared.

There are some other facts about ERT in women who have had a hysterectomy that also need to be brought out in the open. For such women, many physicians prescribe ERT in a cyclic fashion, just as they would for a woman who still has her uterus. And often they will prescribe a progestogen as well. The reason they do this is that they hope this scheme will be more "natural" and that it will be less likely to provoke breast cancer. But the sober facts are that cyclic hormone therapy is not, after all, any more natural than continuous therapy, and—more to the point—there is no firm evidence that ERT increases the overall risk of breast cancer in the first place, or that cycling it or adding a progestogen would help even if it did increase the risk of breast cancer. So both the extra expense and the nuisance of adding the progestogen for part of every month are probably quite unnecessary. Even more important, adding the progestogen may do far more harm than good because it counteracts some of the benefit that ERT has on coronary heart disease.

So you may still be wondering, "What should *I* do?" You should study the facts and make up your own mind. We have given you the facts as they are now known. Remember that the decision you reach doesn't have to be irrevocable. If you decide to start ERT at the time of menopause, you can always stop it anytime you want to. Sometimes you hear people say that if you don't keep it up for five to ten years, it doesn't do you any good. That is nonsense. What they are really saying (or should be saying) is that the benefit that can be derived by short periods of ERT may be relatively small—so small that it is hard to establish with certainty in scientific studies. But that doesn't mean it is not there, or not worth having.

Similarly, don't get stampeded into a decision. If you can't make up your mind for a while, it is surely better not to do something that you will end up fretting about. You can always start ERT later, and you will still derive some benefit. Because most postmenopausal bone loss occurs in the first five years after loss of female hormones, ERT will do you more good if taken early than late. But it still will do you some good, no matter when you start it.

It seems to us that, if you are a woman who has had her uterus removed, the bulk of the evidence tends to favor taking ERT in a low-dosage, everyday schedule, without progestogens, until the age of sixty or sixty-five.

On the other hand, if you still have a uterus, there are good arguments in support of both sides of the decision. *For* ERT is the net gain both in life and in quality of life after balancing off all of the positive and negative effects of ERT on various diseases. *Against* ERT is the medicalization of the menopause—the converting of a normal life event into a disease to be presided over by physicians. Only you can decide which one of those is more important for you.

Incidentally, and to put this issue in a different perspective, if you are a regular smoker, you have chosen to increase your risk of a whole host of potentially fatal diseases to an extent far greater than ERT could, even in the opinions of its strongest critics. We don't think people ought to smoke, but that is not our point in raising the issue here. Rather it is to emphasize that these kinds of choices are not always made logically. Also, it may help you to form a judgement about ERT if you think of it in the same terms as certain other of your life-style choices. Consider a woman who has, over her entire adult life, engaged in chronic dieting, heavy smoking or heavy alcohol use, very little physical work and very limited physical exercise, and the bearing of few or no children. One can often add to these factors a diet since adolescence that is markedly deficient in calcium, and probably in other nutrients as well. It seems less than entirely consistent for this same person to reject ERT at menopause because it is "unnatural." We need to confront and question the integrity of such selective devotion to nature. It seems quite possible that, if all the other factors were optimal, the bone protection afforded by estrogen replacement after menopause might simply not be needed. So while we are critical about the medicalization of the menopause, we cannot totally reject estrogen replacement either. The decision should definitely be an individual one, based on a careful analysis of what is prudent and appropriate to meet the needs of each particular woman in the context of her own life.

32
For Parents

Trends in society—such as participation in competitive sports by increasing numbers of young women, an "attractiveness standard" of extreme thinness, and poor nutrition—can spell poor bone health for your daughters. You can help them develop the habits that build and preserve strong skeletons. We offer practical ways for you, as parents, to educate, encourage, and offer good example.

We may remember our own parents stressing the importance of habits of honesty and hard work. But except for cleanliness and some pretty strange ideas about the importance of regular elimination, they were not very concerned about health habits. Partly this was because not very much was known about the effects of life-style on future health. Partly also this was because up until perhaps fifty years ago, most people in Western society had healthier life-styles than we do today. They got more exercise in the course of everyday activity; they spent more hours out of doors; and working more, they ate more, and hence automatically got more of many essential nutrients. Over the past fifty years there have been massive changes both in standard of living and life-style, probably greater than at any other period in the history of the human race. These changes have important consequences for the future health of every human being. And although these consequences are still being studied, parents who understand some key points can help their children form habits that will benefit them in years to come.

There are many health implications in these life-style changes, and a few have special importance for bone health:

- A decrease in the average amount of physical work or exercise we do every day, particularly after we get a regular job and settle into a work schedule. Runners and joggers are still the exception in our society. Most of us today do far less physical work than did our grandparents.
- A corresponding decrease in the total amount of food we eat, and therefore a decrease in the amount of essential nutrients that we take in.
- A shift in the type of food we eat toward more empty calories—fats, sweets, alcohol. While these foods meet our need for calories, they supply very little of the other essential nutrients.
- An increase in our affluence, which allows us to buy richer, more elegant foods—which often contain less calcium.

These four changes have reduced our calcium intake at precisely the time when we have belatedly come to understand the importance of maintaining a high calcium intake throughout life. For there has been one further change in these past fifty years, a change in scientific understanding that calcium is important throughout life, and especially so during the teens and twenties.

Finally, two other societal changes need to be mentioned.

- Major access to competitive sports for young women.
- A shift in cultural views of attractiveness toward extreme thinness.

These last two have greatly increased the risk that young women will starve themselves until their ovaries stop functioning and they stop having menstrual periods. When this happens, bone loss occurs, just as it does in older women when they lose female hormones at menopause. Whether a young woman is not eating because she wants to be excessively thin or because she wants to run faster or compete at a lower weight in sports, the unfortunate result for her bones can be the same—severe bone loss, even to the point of osteoporotic spine fractures—even while she is still in her twenties.

Given these changes, here are some things parents need to do to protect their daughters and to help them form eating habits that can stay with them throughout life. But first, a word of encouragement to parents. Don't give up. You *can* influence the habits your daughters acquire. All adolescents rebel to some extent. But if you practice good nutrition yourself, and if you explain why these things are important, in most cases your daughters will follow your example and your advice in later years. So here goes:

- Follow good eating habits yourself; get plenty of calcium, and show, in cooking, how to use various calcium-rich foods. Be explicit about this. She needs to know what you are doing and why. This is one of the many things you can teach her.
- Make dairy products available at every meal. If weight is a problem, use skim milk or one of the low-fat milks. Or try nonfat dry milk powder in cooking, or low-fat cheeses, such as Parmesan.
- Find calcium-rich foods your daughter likes and build on them. If she doesn't like liquid milk and simply won't change, don't push. Try yogurt, yogurt-based salad dressings, cheese, and calcium-fortified foods. She will get the message that calcium is important.
- Educate. You teach your children about other things. Teach them about the importance of assuring a good calcium intake—about how they cannot assume they will get enough from today's foods without being aware of their calcium content.
- Stress how important a good calcium intake is, especially during the teens and twenties.
- Be certain you understand how much of different

kinds of foods are required to assure that your daughter gets the RDA for calcium every day. For example, putting milk on your cereal every morning, while a good thing to do, provides probably only 10–20 percent of your calcium requirement.

- Encourage physical exertion in any way your daughter likes. Exercise is good for her skeleton, and by burning calories, it allows her to eat more, and therefore get more of all the essential nutrients in a natural way.

- Be sure she gets regular, *but moderate,* sun exposure. Explain why—because that is how our bodies get the vitamin D they need. If you live in the north, or if your city is cloudy or smoggy a good bit of the time, you may not be able to get enough sun in the winter to make much vitamin D. That is why the dairy industry has fortified both liquid and powdered milk products with vitamin D. You and your daughter can get some of the vitamin D you need that way. But if you are doubtful, a single one-a-day type of multivitamin supplement will give all the vitamin D she—and you —need. But don't overdo it! Too much of certain vitamins can be as harmful as too little, and vitamin D is a good example of that rule.

- Discourage excessive thinness and explain why.

- Don't go along with her in the notion of winning at sports at all costs. The costs to her future health may be too high. Help her to see that.

- Work through your school system to see to it that coaches are not putting hazardous pressures on their players. Many do, and you need to be aware of what they are telling your children. Most coaches know little or nothing about nutrition. Yet they exert great power over the young people they work with.

- See to it that your schools have good nutrition programs. Parents are still the primary source of information for their children, but it is unreasonable to expect you to be experts in everything. In times past, when

most everybody worked hard, ate a lot, grew and pre-
served some of their own food, and weren't rich
enough to afford a lot of empty calories, it was probably easier to be well nourished without worrying
about it. That is no longer true today.

• Examine yourself. Are you overly concerned about
weight loss and thinness? If so, you will transmit your
standards to your daughters. You may not be thin
yourself, but they might become so—even excessively
so. And be careful not to tease them about baby fat.
Be aware, also, that there are genetic differences in fat
distribution among people. You cannot change those
differences by dieting. If you think your thighs are too
heavy, but you are just right everywhere else, and if
you diet until your thighs are what you want them to
be, you will be too thin everywhere else. That is the
way things are. Don't let anybody try to convince you
otherwise.

33
For Children of Aging Parents

*Your mother may already have apparent osteoporosis, or she
may seem to be at risk. We offer several ways you can help her
avoid fractures. We emphasize obtaining and following good
advice, preventing falls and other accidents, communicating
with her physician, and dealing with your own fears and
worries.*

If you have an aging mother or elderly aunts, or if you
have a loved one who has osteoporosis, you may wonder,

"What can I do?" "What should I be telling her?" "How can I help?" We realize that not all parents will take advice from their children, but here are a few pointers that will help you.

Whether or not the person has suffered a fracture as a result of osteoporosis:

- Be certain that she gets enough calcium. It is too late, perhaps, to achieve the skeleton of a thirty-year-old. But a diet generous in calcium can help slow further bone loss. Fifteen hundred milligrams of calcium a day should be a minimum—except in certain rare cases where, for medical reasons, a low calcium intake may be required.

- Encourage regular moderate exercise—walking, a low-impact exercise class, ballroom dancing, or square dancing. Help her find a group of like-minded elderly. The social dimension of the group reinforces the exercise and helps her stick with it.

- Encourage her to use good body mechanics. She should learn how to pick up things off the floor (squat, keeping the back straight—don't bend over), how to lift and carry, and so forth. A nurse may be able to help you greatly here. Certain maneuvers involve a combination of bending and lifting that places great pressure on the spine. Opening the hide-a-bed ought to be recognized as a hazardous activity and left to others. Help her to recognize other, similar activities that she should avoid: taking a heavy turkey out of the oven, trying to open a stuck window, and so on. She should also be careful when putting fitted sheets on the bed.

- Get advice from a physical therapist on back-strengthening exercises and help her to do them regularly. Good, erect posture helps a lot.

- Be certain that she gets enough vitamin D. Most elderly don't get outdoors very much, so it is hard to count on getting vitamin D that way. One or two one-a-day type of multivitamin pills every day would be about right. As we have noted elsewhere, the elderly may need more vitamin D than the young. (But not more than two a day! Too much vitamin D can be as harmful as too little.)

- Help her rearrange her environment to reduce the risk of accident. For example:
  - –Be careful about throw rugs, especially on hardwood floors; even if the rug doesn't slip, it is easy to trip over the edges.
  - –Be certain there is adequate night lighting, to reduce the the risk of falls.
  - –Be certain that there are adequate rails and handholds on stairways and in bathtubs and showers.
- Help her find stable shoes that provide good support. They don't have to be ugly, but spike heels are definitely out for the older woman.
- Be aware that problems related to medications are an important cause of falls. Anything that impairs vision, gait, balance, or level of alertness is a potential hazard. You should be on the alert for medications that make her confused, dizzy, or light-headed. Elderly individuals often react to medications more strongly than do younger people. For example, the bodily systems that break down and eliminate drugs—the liver and kidneys—work less efficiently in older adults. Accordingly, older persons generally need lower dosages. The group of prescription drugs called "major tranquilizers" must be used with great caution by older individuals, because they can cause confusion, blood pressure instability, blackouts, and falls. Other offenders are medications for pain and sleeping pills. Often the elderly are seeing more than one physician, and often they are taking medications that duplicate or enhance one another's effects, or have unexpected interactions. Usually one doctor doesn't know what the other has been prescribing. This is a very common

problem, and while the medical profession ought not to let it happen, the fact of the matter is that they do. So we all need to take some control of this matter for ourselves.

• As another precaution against falls from dizziness, encourage her to take a little extra time when getting up from bed. First, she should sit on the edge for half a minute or so. Then she should stand by the bed for another half minute. By that time her blood pressure control system will have adjusted to the upright posture and she can safely begin to walk around.

If she already has osteoporosis—typically one or more compression fractures of the spine—here are some additional things you can do:

• Talk to her physician, and get her to do so, as well. Find out if the doctor is interested in osteoporosis. If not, find one who is. Physicians are often discouraged by chronic problems like osteoporosis, and sometimes they take a defeatist attitude. That is the last thing you want or need or should tolerate. The patient needs to be encouraged and helped to be as active as possible and to exercise within safe limits (as determined by a competent physician or physical therapist).

• Revise her environment to help her with everyday activities. Nothing she needs should be in bottom drawers or on top shelves, for example. Common sense can help a lot here.

• Get help from an expert occupational therapist or physical therapist on the devices called "aids for daily living." These professionals are expert at helping handicapped people of all sorts, and they can show her how to use devices to pick up things off the floor, reach for things on upper shelves, put on her hose, tie her shoes, and much, much more. The important point is to recognize that these commonplace activities will be hard for her to do, and that there are people and devices who can help her.

- Try to find an osteoporosis support group in your community. If there isn't one, consider starting one yourself. Individuals suffering from osteoporosis and their families can help one another in many ways. To begin with, it is helpful to know that you are not alone, that others have the same problem and are coping with it. Second, you can share coping strategies. Third, you can work together, economically, to get group help from physical therapists (in exercise instruction, for example), from occupational therapists (in aids for daily living), or from nurses. Fourth, osteoporosis tends to isolate people (because they are fearful of injuring themselves or because they are in pain). It is therapeutic just to get them out with other people—but especially with people who understand their problem and can help them to keep it from being too great an intrusion into their lives.

- Finally, keep in mind that you may be dealing with two problems: the health problems of an older adult relative and your own fears and worries. Too much restraint, to allay your own worries, might well make her a virtual prisoner. Of course you want to keep her from falling! But it is good to realize that there are several values to be balanced here.

34

If You Have Osteoporosis

*If you have experienced a fracture attributed to osteoporosis
—typically a compression fracture of the spine—you have a
serious health problem that calls for competent medical care.
However, many women with osteoporosis complain about inadequate information, advice, and treatment from their physicians. We offer commonsense suggestions for recognizing the
right physician and for helping yourself. In the area of posture and body mechanics, we describe certain positions and
motions to avoid, as well as reclining exercises and upright
exercises to do every day.*

If you have had a fracture on minor injury—typically a
sudden, sharp backache that your physician said was due to
compression of one of your vertebrae—you have a medical
condition and you need the care of a competent physician:
someone who knows about osteoporosis, who has had a lot of
experience with people like you, who will take the time to
answer your questions, and who is patient when dealing with
chronic problems such as yours. You need your own physician because, in a book, we cannot practice medicine. We can
tell you about some of the things you need to know, but we
can't diagnose and we can't prescribe—that would be unethi-
cal as well as impractical.

What kind of physician should you look for? There isn't
one right answer to this question, because for every rule we
can give you, we ourselves can cite several exceptions. But
basically you want someone who is patient with chronic

health problems that can't be fixed with a magic bullet, and who has taken the trouble to learn specifically about osteoporosis. There are presently no educational programs in the United States which specifically prepare physicians to specialize in osteoporosis. Instead, some physicians develop a particular interest in osteoporosis *after* they finish formal training. Generally you will find such people among physicians who are trained basically in internal medicine, geriatrics, or physiatry (physical medicine and rehabilitation). Two subspecialties of internal medicine (endocrinology and rheumatology) often harbor physicians interested in osteoporosis. So the kind of physician you want can come from many backgrounds. We know, for instance, of a physician trained as a hematologist (blood specialist) who has shifted his focus to concentrate on osteoporosis.

By contrast, you shouldn't expect to find a lot of help among orthopedic surgeons. Although they are often called "bone specialists," in fact their expertise is mostly in fixing what is broken or in replacing worn-out joints, and they are often very good at that. But most aren't really attuned to your kind of problem. Of course, there are exceptions.

From our correspondence and conversations, it seems that the process of establishing a diagnosis of osteoporosis has often been long and drawn-out—involving several months and even several physicians—after the onset of pain, which is eventually attributed to vertebral collapse. And often, too, what happens after this extended process is merely that a diagnostic label is appended to the woman. She receives no information, no medical advice, no management strategy, really no *care,* in any sense of that word. Let our correspondents speak for themselves.

> Although I consulted both a rheumatologist and an orthopedist, it was four months before a third doctor finally recognized that I was suffering from osteoporosis, causing me to have six broken vertebrae and severe back pain. The orthopedist who recognized the disease prescribed a brace and then dismissed

me. After telling me that my back problem was so severe he could do nothing for me, he sent me to an endocrinologist. . . .

A two-week hospital stay gave me only the name of this ailment.

My doctor doesn't seem too concerned about it. . . .

I have been told by several doctors that I have osteoporosis in my back. Not any of them have given me any medicine or advice.

Perhaps people do not feel free to share their questions and concerns with their physicians. At any rate, it is abundantly clear there is a good deal of dissatisfaction with medical care for the problem. And as we read the hundreds of letters we have received, we many times cannot suppress our own anger at stories that seem to describe unfeeling and incompetent medical management.

It would be easy to turn our dismay into one more diatribe against medicine, but we don't believe that would be useful. We believe there is a deeper reason for patient dissatisfaction than just lack of concern or incompetence on the part of physicians. Understanding that reason may help both you and us in the health professions work toward better care for the victims of all chronic diseases. In simplest terms, there is a very deep mismatch between what society expects of physicians and what they are trained—or temperamentally suited —to provide.

In the last forty years, the profession of medicine has become technology-driven and cure-oriented. It intervenes on behalf of patients when it's possible to do so, but it doesn't help patients help themselves. Physicians are engaged in a battle with disease, with the patient both the battleground and the prize. In chronic, incurable disorders, where it is clear that they cannot win, physicians often are reluctant to play at all. When confronted with such diseases—for example, with all of the manifold disabilities of aging—physicians are generally uncomfortable and all too often feel themselves to be helpless.

It is important to understand this. It is not cynical to say that we will be less disappointed with physicians if we expect less of them. We surely do not mean that persons suffering from osteoporosis should abandon hope. Increasingly we are seeing professional nurses stepping into this gap in our health care system, making up with their unique skills what medicine is not equipped to offer. Nursing is person-oriented, wellness-oriented. It concentrates on patient education, on helping patients and families cope with what cannot be reversed, on preventing complications and reducing disabilities. We believe that there is a real and growing need for nurse-managed osteoporosis centers, in which professional nurses with advanced training would help you cope with existing osteoporosis (and also help young and middle-aged women develop and maintain habits associated with reduced risk).

We also want to call attention to a newly formed organization, the National Osteoporosis Foundation, which was organized both to focus public attention on this disorder and to help patients and families find the help they need and deserve. We expect it to be a source of information about osteoporosis and a national clearinghouse for local self-help and support groups. Its address is 1625 Eye Street, N.W., Suite 1011, Washington, DC 20006. The foundation is compiling a list of osteoporosis specialists countrywide, and they may be able to help you. The foundation is also establishing a network of local chapters. If there is one near you, contact it. They can give you information about physicians in your region and tell you about other resources and programs that may be available to help you. There is great promise in creating the means for patients to share with one another their own successful strategies for coping with the challenges of living with osteoporosis.

Osteoporotic fractures, like other chronic medical conditions, are in the "bad news, good news" category. The bad news is that you have a serious health problem. The good news is that you can probably do something about it. Think of the men you know who have had one coronary attack, recovered, changed their life-styles, and lived happy and productively for many years. The first osteoporotic fracture can be like that. It is bad news, in that you would rather not have had it at all. But it is a chance to change—to help yourself.

It is important to recognize that many compression fractures of the spine are silent. They produce so little discomfort that they are never diagnosed until many years later, when several of them accumulate and back deformity becomes obvious. Often such women have no recollection of backache. One fracture does not condemn you to a life of increasing disability and pain. But it is definitely a call to action.

Here are a few commonsense suggestions that we will go on to explain more fully:

- Work out a treatment program with a physician who understands osteoporosis—and stick to it faithfully.
- Strictly avoid the life-style risk factors for osteoporosis that we talk about in this book.
- Be sure to get enough vitamin D.
- Learn and practice good posture and good body mechanics to protect your back from strain.
- Learn and practice safe strategies for using your bones and strengthening your muscles; for this you should make a plan for walking and exercising every day.
- Don't get discouraged.

Make your needs and wishes clear to your physician, and don't be afraid to be persistent and to ask a lot of questions. Remember, it's your life, your body, your anxiety, your pain, your future (and your money, too). It may be that what you need is a different doctor, a physician who understands osteoporosis and is really interested in working with patients who have this problem. It is vital that you have a physician in whom you have confidence. Don't worry that you may offend your present physician if you are not entirely satisfied.

Treatment at this stage will usually involve:

- estrogen
- a high daily intake of calcium (1.5–3.0 grams; you will probably need to take a supplement to get this much)
- physical therapy, including back muscle strengthening exercises and instruction in proper body mechanics so as to protect weakened vertebrae
- nonnarcotic pain relief (such as aspirin, Tylenol, Advil, or Motrin)

Your physician may also prescribe fluoride. The use of fluoride as a drug in the treatment of osteoporosis is still experimental, but it is being used quite widely. Fluoride shows some promise, but there is still much to be learned about its effectiveness in an osteoporosis treatment program.

Break the habits associated with bone loss and osteoporosis. These include alcohol in excess of one or two drinks each day, smoking, keeping yourself too thin, diets that contain excess protein, and drinking a lot of coffee (more than three cups a day). If you take antacids, you should switch to one of the forms that do not contain aluminum. Read the labels!

Even if you are an older adult (in fact, *especially* if you are), you need vitamin D for healthy bones. As we noted in an earlier chapter, nature's way of getting vitamin D is through moderate exposure of the skin to sunlight (as little as fifteen minutes each day). You can also get vitamin D from a one-a-day type of multivitamin supplement; these generally contain 400 I.U. per tablet, and you can take one or two each day. But if you take vitamin D as a supplement, you should definitely not exceed a daily limit of 1,000 I.U. of vitamin D. As in so many other things concerned with health: not too much, not too little.

Perfect posture and good body mechanics are no longer options for you. They are essential to protect your spine from strain and further damage. You must learn to avoid certain positions and maneuvers, and we illustrate three of them here as EXERCISES TO AVOID.

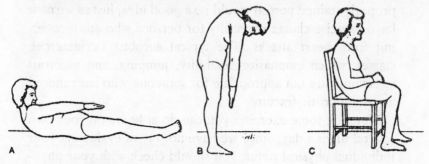

A. AVOID strenuous sit-ups.
B. AVOID toe touches.
C. AVOID slouching when sitting.

You must not do any back-bending exercises. Leaning forward while tugging or lifting is particularly dangerous. It is important to learn the right ways to do housework and lifting. The professional nurse or physical therapist who works with your physician can teach you. Your watchwords should be: stand straight, sit straight, lie straight.

Use a stable, straight chair that has sturdy arms. The arms are useful for supporting your upper body, since you can lean on them with your elbows when your back gets tired. You should also grasp the arms of the chair with your hands to get into and out of the sitting position. The nurse or physical therapist can help you learn these and other maneuvers.

Even though you need to protect your back, you also need exercise and lots of it. In fact, you probably need to engage in a level of exercise that may be completely new for you. If you are to be successful in cutting your chances of further fractures, you must start using your bones and muscles. Walking (with proper athletic shoes or flat-heeled walking shoes, so that you are unlikely to twist an ankle) remains an effective, easy, safe, and enjoyable form of weight-bearing exercise.

Swimming is good because it is exercise, though it may not be weight-bearing in the same way walking is. An exercise class conducted especially for women with osteoporosis by a properly trained person would be a good idea, just as we now have exercise classes especially for persons who are recovering from heart attacks. The typical aerobics or jazzercise classes, which emphasize flexibility, jumping, and vigorous stretching, are not appropriate for someone who has suffered an osteoporotic fracture.

Here are some exercises you can do at home on your own several times a day. Since we have no way of evaluating your individual physical status, you should check with your physician, nurse, or physical therapist before beginning. For reclining exercises, lie on a bed with a firm mattress. Don't try to get down on the floor (it's inconvenient and unnecessary; it can also set the stage for a dangerous fall). Here are instructions for the reclining exercises that we illustrate here.

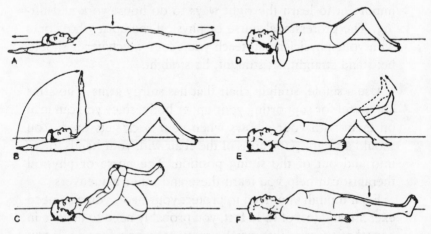

A. Stretch your arms and legs to their greatest length; press your abdomen in to flatten your back in a straight position.

B. With your knees flexed and your back flat, stretch one arm overhead and press it into the bed.

C. Pull your knees up, one at a time, and bring them close to your chest to stretch your lower back.

D. Press your elbows into the bed at right angles to your body.

E. With your back straight and knees bent, straighten and partly flex your knees, one at a time.

F. With your back flat, press your hands and knees down into the bed, contracting your back muscles, buttocks, and thighs.

Here are instructions for the *upright exercises* that we also illustrate.

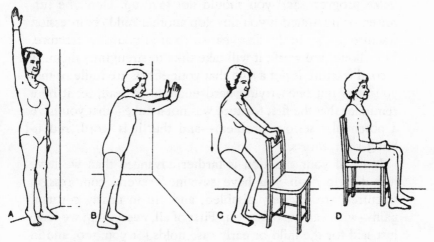

A. Flatten your body against the wall, extend one arm above your head and stretch as high as possible; keep your back flat against the wall.

B. Push off against the wall as you keep your back straight.

C. Partially bend your knees as you keep your back straight.

D. Press your back firmly against a straight chair.

We have borrowed the exercise illustrations and instructions from Dr. Carol Goodman, a specialist in physical medicine and rehabilitation from the Ochsner Clinic in New Orleans.

Certain kinds of foundation garments (but not panty girdles, which can cause circulation problems) can sometimes provide comfortable support of the lower back. Similarly, some women like to wear a posture bra, with wide straps that crisscross in the back. These garments are really matters of individual preference, but some women do find them helpful.

Don't be discouraged if progress seems slow. It has taken many, many years to get you into your present condition. It isn't realistic to expect to get out of it overnight. But you *can* make progress, and you should not give up. Don't be surprised or frustrated if you develop another mild compression fracture or two in the first year or so after your first fracture. Your bones are weak; it will take time to strengthen them. A second fracture is not a sign that your efforts are futile or that you have not been trying hard enough. Instead, let it be a reminder that the first fracture was not a fluke—that you have a potentially serious problem—and that it is worth redoubling your efforts.

Now, if your situation is farther advanced than we have just described—if you have sustained several compression fractures, are severely disabled, and are in nearly constant pain—what can we offer you? First of all, everything we have just said for the mild or early case holds for you, too, and in some instances even more so.

Treatment for osteoporosis is often unsatisfactory. Complete cure is not possible, because the damage that has piled up over the years cannot fully be undone. However real help is possible. It *is* possible to prevent further bone loss, to control pain in most situations, and to deal with complications and disability, even though further fractures may still occur.

Perhaps the single most important advice we can give is to find an interested and able physician. Individuals with advanced osteoporosis are each so different that it would be unwise to try to make general statements. That is why finding the right physician is so important. He or she will be able to deal with you as an individual.

We are often asked about certain forms of treatment, such as the use of orthopedic braces. These are designed to pull the shoulders back and support the upper body weight on the pelvis, and so to relieve stress on the spine. They sound like a good idea, and they seem to work pretty well for young people who have spine problems or have had back surgery, but it has been my experience that they are of very little help to the osteoporotic woman. My patients have spent a lot of money on them over the years, and it has been my impression that they feel this has been money largely wasted.

On the other hand, suppose you've had no fracture, but you have had your bones scanned at one of the many bone-scanning centers that have sprung up around the country, and the scan report claims that you are a high-risk category. Or you have had an X ray taken for some other reason, and the doctor says your bones look "thin." If you have been told any of these things but have not yet sustained a fracture, what should you do? Should you panic? By no means. First of all, the label might well be wrong. We are beginning to hear from women who have come away from the diagnostic centers with a statement that they have osteoporosis, but who probably don't. The simple truth is that any medical diagnosis —including one of osteoporosis—cannot be made with a single test, and high technology and fancy computer printouts do not change that basic truth.

Nevertheless, it should be quite clear by now that, whether your bone mass is dangerously low or not, you should be watching your diet to be certain that you get enough calcium and vitamin D. You should be getting plenty of exercise, and you should be avoiding tobacco and excesses of alcohol and caffeine. If a report from an osteoporosis diagnostic center captures your attention and helps you to focus on these basic health-promoting strategies, then so much the better.

35
No Magic Pill

There is a lot of widely held misinformation about calcium and osteoporosis. Unscrupulous marketing has created the impression that osteoporosis is simply a calcium-deficiency disease. This mistaken notion allows people to ignore many factors known to promote bone deterioration, particularly smoking, drinking, and a sedentary life-style. Also, strategies for preventing osteoporosis have been erroneously touted as cure; although prevention is within grasp, a true cure is not even on the horizon.

Ever since calcium was discovered by the media in 1982, Americans have been subjected to a lot of misinformation. Some is accidental, old ideas left over from the past, disproven but still widely held. We have brought up many of these throughout the book. There are also problems caused by fads, for example the notion that thinness is healthy. Finally, unscrupulous people marketing their own ideas and products (supplements, bone-scanning clinics) have preyed on women's fears.

Advertising has promoted the idea that osteoporosis is solely a calcium-deficiency disease, and that it can be prevented with a pill. It would be nice if things were that simple. But the evidence increasingly indicates that osteoporosis is like other chronic health problems: it probably has its roots early in life; it develops silently over a period of many years; it has multiple causes, including life-style factors and sometimes other diseases; and it finally emerges with the dramatic appearance of a clinical problem—in this case a fracture—in the middle-aged or older adult. This course—which also fits adult-onset diabetes, many kinds of cancers, coronary artery disease, hypertension, and stroke—is typical of chronic diseases generally. For any of these problems, it is a mistake to think of the dramatic event that finally heralds the presence of the disorder as if it were the start of the problem, or to conclude that the problem had just started recently or had a single cause.

We particularly object to the implication that calcium pills can somehow neutralize the many other factors that promote bone deterioration: many nutritional variables, as well as smoking, alcohol abuse, and a sedentary life-style, among others. It is quite clear that bones must be used or they will be lost, and yet no ad emphasizes the necessity of physical work or exercise.

The idea that there is some magic pill to cure osteoporosis is nourished by enthusiastic and often premature reports of breakthroughs in the popular press. As an example, when the American Society for Bone and Mineral Research released its general guidelines for osteoporosis prevention in 1982—encouraging moderate exercise and adequate calcium intake over the adult life span—the headlines of some newspapers announced a "cure." What a sad distortion of the truth!

Before American lives became medicalized, people did not expect drugs or surgery to reverse years of neglect. Antibiotics and improved public health measures had not begun to conquer infectious disease. Great emphasis was placed upon exercise, fresh air, sunshine, good nutrition, adequate rest, and so on—the "grandmother's advice" that science is showing still to be wise. People took responsibility for their own well-being. Now, with the capacity of modern, technology-based medicine to offer dramatic fixes for at least some health problems (for example, bypass surgery for coronary artery disease), we have mistakenly assumed that it can do everything for us. We have gradually lost—and are only beginning to regain—a sense of personal responsibility for our own well-being. There is still a lot of self-deception—or maybe ignorance—about the bad effects of smoking, alcohol abuse, poor eating habits, lack of activity, and so on.

Remarkably little attention has been paid to smoking as a women's health issue. This is really quite a remarkable omission, for smoking is irrefutably a multifaceted health hazard. The evidence is overwhelming: for the respiratory system (lung cancer, aggravation of allergies, and emphysema), for pregnancy (low birth weight, prematurity, respiratory problems in the newborn, and even stillbirths), for the cardiovascular system (hypertension, stroke, and coronary artery disease), for the skin (wrinkles, dryness, and early aging), and for other cancers (esophagus, larynx, stomach, bowel, urinary bladder, and breast). In addition, as we have noted, smoking promotes bone loss and thus the development of osteoporosis. We wonder how *any* smoker can expect to escape every one of these health impairments.

The evidence is overwhelmingly in favor of prevention as the most hopeful strategy for all the chronic diseases. If you understand the multicausal nature and the long, insidious course of chronic illnesses before they become evident, then you can see that hope for cure by a single medication or medical procedure is unrealistic. Of course we believe that better methods for managing and treating osteoporosis (and other chronic illnesses) should continue to be sought. But we do want to draw a distinction between treatment and cure, between—for example—better methods for pain control (treatment) and actual replacement of lost bone structure (cure). The one is within our grasp. The other is not even on our horizon.

Be wary of miracle solutions to complex problems. Be a critical—though not cynical—reviewer of what you hear and see and of what others say and sell.

In this book we have stressed understanding—understanding of how bone health comes about, of what calcium nutrition consists of and how it influences bone health, and of many other seeming details. The reason we have done this is because, with understanding, you can exercise a measure of control over what happens to you and to your loved ones.

Some people don't want the responsibility or the control. We hear women say: "Well, if I get osteoporosis, I will just get it . . . there is nothing I can do about it"—as if it were only a matter of chance. That is not true. The facts are that, even though responsibility *is* fuzzy and control *is* incomplete, still you can take much of the responsibility and assume much of the control. The truth is: Prudence pays off.

Furthermore, the prudent steps we have outlined are all fairly simple things to do—good diet, sunshine, exercise, avoidance of smoking and of excesses of alcohol. You have to know *how* to do them, of course, because, while simple, they are not obvious. And you need to know *why* they are important; otherwise you might not stick with them. But still, they are simple enough to do, once you understand.

That, in a perverse way, may be a disadvantage. People seem more willing to try something bizarre or burdensome than something simple. In the second book of Kings is the story of Naaman, who was irritated by being instructed to wash seven times in the river Jordan. It was too simple a thing to do for something as serious as his leprosy—and for someone as important as a Syrian general. But his servants reminded him that, if Elisha had asked him to do something hard, he would have done it. All the more reason, they said, to do the simple thing he prescribed.

Appendix:
Calcium and Life

THE CALCIUM AROUND US

Calcium is the fifth most abundant element in the earth's crust, more prevalent than any element except oxygen, silicon, aluminum, and iron. Calcium compounds make up the chalk we use to write on blackboards, the plaster covering our walls, and much of the stone of our buildings. A calcium compound, lime, was the principal component of the mortar that was used for centuries to hold building blocks together. In combination with magnesium and other elements, calcium forms dolomite, the substance of whole mountain ranges. Calcium is the principal mineral in the stalagmites and stalactites of caves. It makes drinking water hard and causes boiler scale in hot water and steam heating systems. Calcium is the stuff of marble, coral, pearls, seashells, eggshells, and teeth. Most important for our purposes, calcium is the mineral of bones.

What *is* calcium? It is one of the ninety-two chemical elements that make up the earth and everything on it. All the calcium on earth was made at the time our galaxy was formed. Calcium is neither made nor destroyed today, either within our bodies or elsewhere. (The one exception is in nuclear reactors and nuclear explosions.) The earth has as much calcium as it had 15 or so billion years ago. Like most other elements, calcium forms chemical compounds with other elements. This is how we encounter calcium in our bones, in our foods, and in calcium supplements.

The calcium atom, like all atoms, consists of a central nucleus containing positively charged particles, surrounded by an equal number of negatively charged particles called electrons that are arranged in orbiting shells. The outer shell of electrons, in the case of calcium, contains two electrons; but calcium, like other metals, tends to lose these outer electrons to certain other elements that bind them more tightly. A calcium atom missing these two negative charges is a positively charged calcium ion.

Calcium ions, being positively charged, readily form complexes with negatively charged ions, forming electrically balanced, or neutral, complexes with equal numbers of positive and negative charges. Such compounds of positive and negative ions are called "salts." Table salt, or sodium chloride, is the most familiar of the huge class of salts. (In table salt, sodium is the positive ion and chloride the negative ion.)

The chemical compounds of calcium that surround us include calcium oxide occurring as lime; calcium carbonate in the form of chalk, limestone, marble, seashells, and pearls; and calcium phosphate in bones and teeth. The calcium in milk and other dairy products is in the form of calcium citrate and calcium phosphate. There are hundreds of other calcium salts, some manmade, but most natural. Calcium supplements are basically nothing more than calcium salts (see Chapter 27).

The general abundance of calcium means that there is a lot of calcium in most soils in which plants grow, in the ocean, and in most freshwater lakes and streams. Calcium is essential for life as we know it. Most plants will not grow in calcium-poor soil, and freshwater streams low in calcium do not support much life. There are many reasons for this. Calcium is vital for the activities of living cells, as we will explore in the next section. But also, calcium helps to keep carbon dioxide dissolved in water. Carbon dioxide is the basic building block that all plants use for building complex molecules through photosynthesis. Plants living on land get carbon dioxide through the air, but aquatic plants can get it only through carbon dioxide dissolved in the water. Single-celled, photosynthetic plants are at the bottom of the food chain for all aquatic life forms. At this basic level calcium and life are inextricably linked.

CALCIUM AND LIFE PROCESSES

Three billion years ago, as living forms evolved in the brackish estuaries of our planet, they began to build upon, to take advantage of, to incorporate somehow the calcium that was everywhere. Other even more common elements, such as silicon and aluminum, were largely ignored. Science fiction writers speculate about what life might have been like had evolution taken an alternate path at this point—chosen silicon, for instance, instead of calcium. We shall never know. Life took the calcium route. From that point on, there has been an intimate partnership between calcium and the molecules of life.

On the chemical scale of things, certain of the molecules of life—proteins—are usually huge affairs, with hundreds of thousands of atoms, mostly carbon, hydrogen, oxygen, and nitrogen. The atoms are arranged in complex, folded chains of building blocks called amino acids. Unlike the salts, which consist of ions of opposite charge attracted to one another electrically, the atoms that make up protein molecules are all neutral, bonded together by sharing the electrons of their outer shells. But even though neutral overall, some regions of protein molecules are more negative and others more positive. This surface distribution of charge has important influences on the properties and activities of the molecules of life.

Among other things, some of these molecules can reproduce themselves, and others, called enzymes, can extract energy from other molecules or otherwise change them. Like tools in a workshop, enzymes work as drills or saws or welders. But unlike workshop machines, these biological machines are very specific about what they will work on. For example, the enzymes that split other proteins into smaller pieces will work only on certain links within a protein chain. So instead of one or two all-purpose saws, typical organisms have hundreds of enzymes, each working on slightly different materials. So, too, typical organisms have hundreds of highly specific joining enzymes that put different parts together to produce new molecules.

Where does calcium come into this picture? Enzymes are suspended in protoplasm, the watery stuff of living cells. In this liquid, many enzyme molecules are floppy or limp, assuming a variety of shapes, often crucially different from the shape that enables them to work as tools. They adopt and maintain that crucial shape only when certain other substances—mostly metal ions—bind to them. The metal ion fits into a fold or crevice of the protein structure; its positive charge attracts negative regions of the large protein molecule and draws them together to shape and stiffen the enzyme. Now it can act.

Which metal ions work better for which enzymes depends upon the size of the ion, its net charge, and the dimensions of the cavity in the protein. Calcium ions are of just the right shape and charge to fit into many of the most basic enzyme molecules. Calcium is the key that turns them on. No other element will do.

But there is a problem here. With so much calcium around, enzymes might be working all the time, like a workshop with all the tools running at one time. They might even attack one another. This powerful key must be controlled.

In primitive, single-celled organisms, a skin or membrane separates the biological machinery within the cell from the outside world. Mechanisms have evolved to control what passes in and out through the membrane. Some of these are gates that open and close; others are pumps that pull in what is needed and push out what is not. Calcium is one of the substances that are pushed out. In this way the concentration of calcium in the water inside a cell ends up being only about one one-millionth the concentration in the outside environment, and, under resting conditions, the cell machinery is idling. Then, when a cell needs certain enzymes in an active form, the gates are opened to let calcium pour in. The crucial enzymes are activated, and the specific job performed. To turn the system off, the cell pumps the calcium back out, returning its molecular machinery to an idling state.

As cells became more complicated and diversified, just letting the calcium pour in from outside became inefficient. For a big cell the process might take too long to permit a quick response. To prevent this, many cells evolved internal storage compartments. There they keep calcium safely stored away when it is not activating enzymes such as those involved in muscle contraction. In addition to muscle contraction, what are some of the other vital processes initiated by calcium? One is blood coagulation, the result of a complex series of enzyme reactions in which a crucial step requires calcium. Another involves the response that virtually all cells make to external messages or signals. In large, complex, multicellular organisms, both plants and animals, the billions of cells that go to make up an individual need to communicate, so as to coordinate their activities. Nerve impulses and hormones are the main signals the body uses to coordinate its parts. With both, the message is received at the cell surface, and its effect is to let calcium concentration rise in crucial locations within the cell, triggering a cascade of biochemical reactions which ultimately result in the cell doing its thing. The first messenger is the chemical or nervous impulse received from outside the cell; calcium is a kind of universal second messenger, translating that first message into the specific cellular actions.

In a complex, multicellular organism, there is also a need to regulate the level of calcium *outside* the cell, in the kind of internal sea that bathes living tissues. The reasons the extracellular calcium must be regulated are quite different from those we have just described, and we will examine them in the next section. This regulation of extracellular calcium is, if

anything, even more pertinent to the questions which are at
the center of this book—that is, calcium and health. The calcium within our cells is so basic to life processes that cells
jealously hang onto their calcium. There are no disorders
currently recognized by medicine in which there is abnormal
regulation of the calcium within cells. It is both interesting
and useful to understand this intimate link between calcium
and the basic life processes. However, the disorders of calcium nutrition relate to the control of calcium *around* the
cells, rather than *within* them.

WHERE CALCIUM IS LOCATED IN OUR BODIES

An adult man has about 1,000–1,200 grams of calcium in
his body, and an adult woman, about 800–900 grams. (This
is roughly 2.25–2.50 pounds of calcium for a man and 1.75–
2.0 pounds for a woman.) The calcium is in three places.
Ninety-nine percent of the body's calcium is in the skeleton.
The remaining 1 percent—roughly eight to nine grams—is in
the soft tissues of our bodies (liver, muscle, brain, etc.).
Seven to eight of these nine grams are distributed through all
the cells of the body; this is the calcium that is vital to the
basic cell functions. The other one gram or so is dissolved in
the extracellular fluid (ECF), which includes the blood
plasma and bathes every cell of the body.

Most of the organs and tissues of the body consist mainly of
living cells. There is a little bit of space between those cells,
filled with the internal sea we have been calling extracellular
fluid. This extracellular fluid is both within the blood and
around the cells. The body goes to great lengths to regulate
the level of many critical elements in this internal sea. Further, there is a lot of it—roughly 15 percent of body weight is
accounted for by this liquid that pervades all of our tissues
and organs.

By studying a sample of blood, we can measure what is
going on in the extracellular fluid. The blood, of course, cir-

culates and thereby ties all the remote regions of the extracellular fluid together, mixes with and feeds them, replenishes what each region has consumed, and takes away what it no longer needs. When we talk about calcium in the extracellular fluid, we might just as well talk about calcium in the blood, for that is what we measure. Still, the extracellular fluid is more than the blood; it is what the cells "see."

As we noted earlier, cells hang on to their calcium tenaciously. It is essential for their survival. They don't rely upon being supplied by the rest of the organism, nor do they share their calcium with other cells. Medicine does not yet recognize any diseases which alter this within-cell calcium. However, some scientists now believe that certain types of high blood pressure may be the result of just such a disorder.

In any case, when we speak of calcium and health, we are most concerned with the calcium dissolved in the water around our cells (the extracellular fluid) and the calcium in our bones. These two locations interact in important ways.

The calcium in the extracellular fluid, though accounting for only 0.1 percent of the total calcium in the body, plays a crucial role in the coordination of tissues and organs. As we have already noted, the cells have to coordinate their activities. The most important way they communicate is through the nervous system—not only the nerves that mediate conscious, voluntary activity, but also those that control involuntary activity such as heart rate, blood pressure, and digestion.

In each case, a long nerve cell fiber, almost like an electrical wire, carries the message. Its end comes into very close contact with the surface of one or more cells to be controlled —for example, muscle cells in the thigh, the intestinal wall, or in the wall of an artery, or special cells that produce gastric juice, or even other nerve cells. When a nerve cell conducts a signal, it produces chemical substances precisely at the point of contact with its target cells, and these chemical substances diffuse very rapidly across the ultramicroscopic gap between the cells to stimulate the target cells. But a target cell doesn't always respond; sometimes it seems to ignore the signal. This is because there wasn't enough of the chemical substance released by the nerve to evoke a response—to get over the "firing threshold" of the target cell. Sometimes the cell has raised its threshold so that even a stimulus of moderate intensity won't produce a reaction.

The concentration of calcium in the water that fills the tiny gap between the two cells is crucial to the response of the target cell. The gaps between nerve and muscle cell, for example, are part of the extracellular fluid. The optimal concentration of calcium in the extracellular fluid compartment is about four to five milligrams per 100 milliliters. This is about the level of calcium in many of the freshwater streams and lakes that support abundant aquatic life. Many scientists believe that multicellular life forms evolved in just such an environment, and further that mechanisms for intracellular communication were adapted to the calcium level prevailing in those waters.

Organisms that left the primordial aquatic environment had to regulate the concentration of many substances in their internal fluid. Calcium is one of those substances, and we know that intracellular communication becomes seriously disturbed whenever calcium levels change even slightly.

In simple terms, when the level of calcium falls too low, the target cells—particularly muscle cells—tend to fire too easily. Even a very gentle nervous stimulus can evoke a massive response. Thus, if the calcium level in the extracellular fluid is too low, rigidity, muscle spasms, and even convulsions occur.

At the other extreme, when calcium rises too high, limpness, poor muscle tone, severe constipation, and fatigue occur. At extremely high levels, virtually all communication involving nerve cells ceases; unconsciousness ensues, and the heart stops beating altogether. (This almost never happens by itself, and is mostly found in extremely severe types of endocrine tumors, or in advanced vitamin D poisoning.)

This relaxation—actually a total shutdown of almost all muscle contraction—may seem a strange result of too much calcium, inasmuch as we have just seen that calcium activates the contractile proteins. One might have expected, therefore, just the opposite: constant contraction at high levels of calcium in the extracellular fluid, and inactivity at low levels. But that's confusing the calcium *inside* the cells with the calcium *around* them. Outside, or extracellular, calcium affects cell-to-cell communication. As we have seen, the cells regulate their own internal levels, which are quite independent of fluctuations in calcium outside the cell. No one yet knows for certain exactly how calcium influences cell-to-cell transmission, but the effects are clear enough.

Any departure from optimal calcium levels in the extracellular fluid interferes with the communication between cells that is necessary for the coordinated functioning of multicellular organisms. For that reason it is not surprising that mechanisms have evolved to keep calcium levels in the extracellular fluid within those very narrow limits. These mechanisms are not only of paramount importance to good health, but they also affect the very large body of calcium that exists in the skeleton.

Many biologists believe that the basic role of bone is not as a structural or supporting tissue at all, but as a reservoir of calcium and phosphorus. With an internal reserve, organisms become independent of day-to-day or season-to-season fluctuations in calcium level in the surrounding aquatic environment. This very primitive role of bone has never been lost. It remains significant, even for human beings, as we shall see.

Nevertheless, we tend to think of bone mainly in mechanical terms. A skeleton gives us shape and rigidity. It makes it possible for us to lift and carry, to reach and jump. Fish don't really need bone for structural support the way we do, because they are supported externally by the water. But when organisms crawled out onto dry land they had to provide some system of support (exoskeletons in the case of insects, endoskeletons in the case of most other land animals). Bone —already existing as a buffer for fluctuations in calcium level in the extracellular fluid—was recruited to serve a new purpose, mechanical support.

Evolutionary biology is filled with examples of compounds, structures, and even functions that evolved for one purpose and in more advanced organisms have adapted to other purposes. But often—as in the case of bone—the primitive purpose is never lost, even if it becomes less obvious. In the case of the skeleton, bone still functions as a reservoir of calcium. If there is loss of calcium from the critical extracellular fluid, the organism will tear down bone to scavenge the calcium it contains. Indeed, this scavenging process will continue until the bone is so weak that it can no longer support the body.

Thus, the extracellular fluid, which contains only 0.1 percent of all the calcium in the body, exerts *the* dominant influence on the skeleton, which contains about 99 percent of the body's calcium.

Glossary

Note: Words that are in italics are also listed as separate entries.

ABSORPTION EFFICIENCY: The fraction of the calcium present in an individual's diet that passes from the intestine into the bloodstream; young adults typically absorb about 25–35 percent of the calcium they ingest; absorption efficiency varies among individuals and falls with advancing age.

ANOREXIA NERVOSA: An eating disorder; young women with anorexia nervosa severely limit their intake of food, which leads to drastic weight loss, cessation of ovarian activity, serious health impairment, and early loss of *bone mass.*

BIOAVAILABILITY: The intestinal absorbability of calcium as present in a specific food item or *calcium supplement;* whereas the calcium in dairy products is readily available for absorption, the calcium in most foods and supplements has not been measured; for supplements, bioavailability has two components—whether the tablets break up in the stomach, and whether the calcium compound they contain is absorbed.

BONE ARCHITECTURE: The microscopic structure of *trabecular bone* that makes it more or less strong and able to support the weight of the body.

BONE FORMATION: The final stage in the process of *bone remodeling; osteoblasts* manufacture and secrete the components of *bone matrix,* which then draw the components of *bone mineral* from the bloodstream to produce new hard tissues.

BONE MASS: The amount of bone that makes up the skeleton; bone mass is influenced by heredity, nutrition, and physical work, and is typically greatest (peak bone mass) between the ages of thirty and forty.

BONE MATRIX: The *protein* component of bone, which gives bone its elastic character and makes up about half the volume of bone and one third its weight; see also *collagen.*

BONE MINERAL: The crystalline component of bone, which gives bone its rigid character; calcium and phosphorus (in the form of hydroxyapatite) are the principal components of bone mineral.

BONE REMODELING: The microscopic process of renewal and repair in bone in which specialized cells—*osteoclasts* and *osteoblasts*—excavate bone and replace it with *bone matrix* and *bone mineral.*

BONE RESORPTION: An early stage in the process of bone remodeling; *osteoclasts* excavate microscopic pits in *trabecular bone* or tunnels in *cortical bone* in response to an activation signal; *bone formation* then usually takes place at these same sites.

BONE SCAN: Procedure for measuring *bone mass* and *bone mineral* density in living persons; an instrument called a dual-photon absorptiometer (DPA) is used for bone scans of the spine, hip, and total body; a single-photon absorptiometer (SPA) is used to scan the heel and wrist; a type of computer tomography (CT) is used to scan the center of individual vertebrae; bone scanning is a research procedure with limited value in the care of individual patients.

BULIMIA: An eating disorder; young women with bulimia have repeated cycles of binge-and-purge, in which they ingest large quantities of food and then make themselves vomit; bulimia is a serious threat to health, even though extreme weight loss may not take place.

CAFFEINE: The chemical component of coffee and tea that acts as a stimulant; caffeine is added to cola beverages and to certain prescription and nonprescription drugs; an individual who ingests caffeine has a higher individual calcium *requirement* than one who does not.

CALCITONIN: A small *protein hormone* produced in the thyroid gland; calcitonin acts on *osteoclasts* to reduce *bone resorption* and thereby to reduce or prevent elevations of calcium in the *extracellular fluid.*

CALCIUM ABSORPTION: See *absorption efficiency.*

CALCIUM SUPPLEMENT: Calcium in concentrated chemical form and ingested as a medication, as distinguished from *dietary calcium.*

CANCELLOUS BONE: See *trabecular bone.*

COLLAGEN: The principal *protein* component of bone, as well as of cartilage, ligaments, tendons, and skin; collagen is a long, fibrous protein, laid down in multiple plywoodlike layers in bone; see also *bone matrix* and *connective tissue.*

COMPACT BONE: See *cortical bone.*

CONNECTIVE TISSUES: Parts of the body that consist principally of extracellular material, including bone, cartilage, ligaments, tendons, and skin; *collagen* is the principal component of all connective tissues.

CORTICAL BONE: The dense form of bone that makes up the shafts of long bones (the humerus, radius, and ulna of the arm and the femur, tibia, and fibula of the leg) and the outer walls of other bones.

CRUSH FRACTURE: See *vertebral fracture.*

DIETARY CALCIUM: Calcium ingested in food; the dietary calcium of the vast majority of adolescent girls and adult women in the United States is insufficient to build and sustain a strong skeleton.

ENZYME: A specialized *protein* that acts as a catalyst in a chemical reaction within living organisms; calcium converts many enzymes into their active forms.

ESTROGEN: A class of hormones produced principally by the ovaries and responsible for the development of distinctively female body characteristics; the ovaries produce estrogen until natural or surgical *menopause;* see also *estrogen replacement therapy.*

ESTROGEN REPLACEMENT THERAPY (ERT): The use of *estrogen* (in tablets or other forms) after the *menopause* to relieve discomfort, preserve *bone mass,* and prevent cardiovascular disease; ERT has advantages and disadvantages, benefits and risks, which should be evaluated on an individual basis.

EXTRACELLULAR FLUID: The fluid, including blood plasma, which bathes all the cells of the body and makes up their chemical environment; the level of calcium in the extracellular fluid is maintained by the body within narrow limits by elaborate *hormone*-mediated control systems.

FIBER: A component of vegetable foods that is usually indigestible; dietary fiber promotes good bowel function, but excess fiber increases the individual *requirement* for calcium by decreasing calcium *absorption efficiency.*

FLUORIDE: A chemical element used as a drug in some treatment plans for individuals with osteoporosis; basically the same substance as is used in water fluoridation and in many toothpastes.

FRACTURE: Structural failure of bone following the application of force (synonym: broken bone); in *osteoporosis,* bones may become so weak that trivial injuries or even ordinary activities lead to structural failure, especially *vertebral fracture* and *hip fracture.*

FRACTURE ZONE: The group of bone mass values low enough for fracture to occur as a result of trivial injuries or even ordinary activities; when postmenopausal bone loss occurs rapidly or proceeds from an inadequate peak *bone mass,* a woman's skeleton is said to enter the fracture zone.

HIP FRACTURE: Structural failure of the upper end of the thighbone (femur); hip fracture usually occurs in one of two areas, just below the head of the femur or through a wider region a little lower down (the "intertrochanteric" zone); hip fracture is an important cause of disability, dependence, and death in elderly women.

HYSTERECTOMY: Surgical removal of the uterus (womb); surgical removal of the ovaries (oophorectomy or ovariectomy) may or may not accompany hysterectomy; see also *menopause.*

HORMONE: A substance produced by specialized cells in one of the endocrine organs and released into the bloodstream; hormones are chemical messengers that act on cells distant from those in which they are made; the pituitary, thyroid, parathyroid, kidney, pancreas, adrenal, ovary, and testis are all endocrine organs that produce hormones.

INTRACELLULAR CALCIUM: The calcium within living cells, where it is principally used to activate *enzymes;* when not in use, this calcium is stored in special microscopic enclosures within the cells, so that the level of dissolved intracellular calcium is extremely low.

ION: An atom in which one or more electrons have been lost or gained; thus an ion has a positive or negative charge; many elements exist in nature as ions, usually combined with other ions of opposite charge; calcium exists in living organisms as an ion lacking two of its electrons, and so is positively charged.

MENOPAUSE: Permanent cessation of ovarian function; natural menopause occurs when the ovaries stop producing estrogen at about the age of fifty to fifty-three; surgical menopause occurs when both ovaries are removed in a surgical operation, often at the time of *hysterectomy.*

MICRODAMAGE: An effect of wear and tear on bone as a structural material and consisting of tiny cracks ordinarily repaired through *bone remodeling;* if it accumulates, microdamage can lead to *fracture* upon minor trauma.

MORTALITY: Another term for death, especially in research reports that describe statistics on large groups of individuals (populations).

OBLIGATORY LOSS: The amount of the body's store of calcium that always escapes from the body each day in urine, feces, sweat, dead skin, and so on; obligatory loss must be replaced from the diet or the body will tear down bone to scavenge its calcium.

OSTEOBLAST: A specialized cell that forms new bone; osteoblasts secrete the components of *bone matrix* in the final stage of *bone remodeling.*

OSTEOCLAST: A very large specialized cell that tears down old bone by excavating microscopic pits and tunnels in an early stage of *bone remodeling.*

OSTEOCYTE: A cell within the structure of bone, part of a network of such cells nourished by blood vessels; living osteocytes are essential for the function of the bone remodeling apparatus, perhaps by activating *osteoclasts* at sites of *microdamage.*

OSTEOMALACIA: A disease in which areas of *bone matrix* fail to attract bone mineral; osteomalacia can be caused by many factors, but is regularly produced by severe deficiency of *vitamin D* in adults.

OSTEOPOROSIS: A chronic disease occurring predominantly in women and characterized by the development of low *bone mass* and structural failure of the skeleton (for example, *vertebral fracture* or *hip fracture)* in response to trivial injury.

OXALATE (OXALIC ACID): A chemical substance found in certain foods that binds calcium tightly and reduces its *bioavailability;* oxalate-rich foods (such as spinach and rhubarb) are not useful dietary sources of calcium.

PARATHYROID HORMONE (PTH): A small *protein hormone* produced by four tiny endocrine glands in the neck, which influences the *absorption efficiency* of calcium, the rate of *bone remodeling,* and the loss of calcium in the urine.

PROGESTOGEN: A class of *hormones* produced by the ovaries and responsible for preparing the lining of the uterus to support pregnancy.

PROTEIN: A class of large, complex chemical compounds produced by living organisms and made up of chains of subunits called amino acids; proteins are also essential nutrients needed for the growth and repair of organs and tissues throughout the body; excess dietary protein increases the individual *requirement* for calcium.

RECOMMENDED DIETARY ALLOWANCE (RDA): The quantity of an essential nutrient which, when ingested in the daily diet, will meet the needs of about nineteen out of every twenty individuals; the remaining one in twenty actually requires more than the RDA; RDAs for the various nutrients are established and revised on a periodic basis by the National Research Council; many scientists believe that the official RDA for calcium is set too low to meet the needs of most women.

RELATIVE RISK: A number that expresses how much a person's chances of contracting a disorder are affected by some exposure or condition; thus an alcoholic woman has a relative risk for osteoporosis of 10, or ten times the risk of a woman who is not an alcoholic; an obese woman has a relative risk for osteoporosis of 0.3, or only three tenths the risk of a woman of average weight.

REQUIREMENT: The quantity of a specific nutrient needed by an individual to maintain health; the individual requirement for calcium in women is influenced by *estrogen* status (that is, whether or not estrogen is present), calcium *absorption efficiency, vitamin D* status, and dietary habits; excessive intakes of *protein, caffeine, sodium,* or *fiber* all increase the individual requirement for calcium.

RICKETS: A disease of children marked by defective *bone formation* and severe skeletal deformities; rickets is often due to deficiency of *vitamin D.*

RISK FACTOR: An exposure or condition that increases the likelihood that an individual will develop a particular health problem; risk factors for osteoporosis include heredity (such as positive family history, petite build, and fair skin), life-style factors (such as poor dietary habits, smoking, and low activity level), and certain other health problems (and treatment regimens) that favor poor bone development and/or bone loss.

SODIUM: A chemical element that enters the diet chiefly in the form of table salt (sodium chloride); excess dietary sodium increases the individual requirement for calcium; sodium-restricted diets are often also low in calcium.

TRABECULAR BONE: The spongy-appearing form of bone that fills the ends of long bones and constitutes a significant fraction of the central parts of the *vertebrae;* trabecular bone has a system of interconnecting cross-braces somewhat like an egg crate, and if these braces are thinned or lost, trabecular bone is weakened.

VERTEBRA (plural, VERTEBRAE): An individual bone in the spine; each vertebra has a central portion (the vertebral body), a bony arch encasing the spinal cord, and several projections (for muscle attachment); vertebral fractures in osteoporosis always involve only the body of the vertebra, and not the other portions.

VERTEBRAL FRACTURE: Structural failure of a bone in the spine, typically following loss of bone mass and weakening of the vertebrae after *menopause;* collapse of a vertebral body is called a crush fracture, and partial collapse is called a wedge fracture (because the vertebral body becomes wedge-shaped); repeated fractures result in a loss of height and the characteristic back deformity called dowager's hump (kyphosis).

VITAMIN: A nutrient needed in trace amounts for health but which cannot be made by the human body; vitamins are made by other living organisms and taken into the human body as food.

VITAMIN D: A substance which increases an individual's capacity to absorb *dietary calcium* (see *absorption efficiency)* and which has other effects as well, particularly in bone; vitamin D is not actually a true vitamin, since it is produced in the human body when skin is exposed to sunlight; nevertheless it has for so long been grouped with the true vitamins that the name "vitamin" is now permanently attached to it.

Resources

CALCIUM AND BONES

FOR THE GENERAL READER

Heaney, R. P., and G. D. Whedon. "Bone." *Encyclopedia Britannica*, 1978.

SCIENTIFIC BACKGROUND

Heaney, R. P., and M. J. Barger-Lux. "Calcium, Bone Metabolism, and Structural Failure." *Triangle: The Sandoz Journal of Medical Science* 23:91–100, 1985.
> This paper takes a broad perspective on the relationship of calcium to age-related loss of bone integrity for the scientific audience.

Recker, R. R., P. D. Saville, and R. P. Heaney. "The Effect of Estrogens and Calcium Carbonate on Bone Loss in Postmenopausal Women." *Annals of Internal Medicine* 87:649–655, 1977.
> A study showing how supplements can slow bone loss in some regions of the skeleton, but not others.

CALCIUM AS A NUTRIENT

FOR THE GENERAL READER

Consumer Guide Calcium Counter to Basic Foods and Brand Names. New York: Signet, 1986 (160 pages).
> This inexpensive paperback lists the amounts of calcium in servings of natural, processed, and fast foods, with listings according to brand names.

"A Hard Act to Follow: Getting More Calcium." *Tufts University Diet Nutrition Letter* 2:3, July 1984.

Hausman, P. *The Calcium Bible: How to Have Better Bones All Your Life.* New York: Warner Books, 1985 (205 pages).
> Written by a nutritionist, this book contains a great collection of dietary strategies for increasing calcium intake, including forty-one pages of recipes and suggestions for individuals on special diets.

HEALTH-AIDE. Software from Programming Technology, 7 San Marcos Place, San Rafael, CA 94901.

This is the software used in our research unit for diet analysis. It runs on the Apple IIe or IBM-PC, and should be useful to the home computer user who wants to do computer-supported analysis of diets for calories, vitamins, and minerals (including calcium).

Hecht, A. "Calcium: More Than Just the Strong Stuff of Bones." *FDA Consumer* 15:14, July/August 1981.

From the National Dairy Council (6300 North River Road, Rosemont, IL 60018):

The All-American Guide to Calcium-Rich Foods, 1984.

"Calcium Absorption and Requirements During the Life Span." *Nutrition News* 47(1), February 1984.

Calcium—You Never Outgrow Your Need for It, 1984.

National Dairy Council Catalog of Nutrition Education Materials.

"The Role of Calcium in Bone Health." *Nutrition News* 47(2), April 1984.

SCIENTIFIC BACKGROUND

Carroll, M. D., S. Abraham, and C. M. Dresser. *Dietary Intake Source Data, United States, 1976–1980.* Hyattsville, Maryland: National Center for Health Statistics, 1983. DHHS publication no. (PHS) 83–1681. (Data from national health survey series 11, no. 231).
This is HANES-II, the authoritative source book for what Americans actually eat.

Eaton, S. B., and M. Konner. "Paleolithic Nutrition." *New England Journal of Medicine* 312(5):283–289, 1985.
A fascinating study of what may have been the nutrition of the first true humans.

Heaney, R. P. "Calcium, Bone Health, and Osteoporosis." In: *Bone and Mineral Research,* W. A. Peck, ed., annual 4, pp. 255–301. Science Publishers, Amsterdam: Elsevier, 1986.
A very detailed, comprehensive, and extensively documented review of the relationship between calcium intake and bone health.

Heaney, R. P., R. R. Recker, and P. D. Saville. "Calcium Balance and Calcium Requirements in Middle-Aged Women. *American Journal of Clinical Nutrition* 30:1603–1611, 1977.
This paper was the first to show the importance of adequate calcium intake in middle-aged women.

Heaney, R. P., R. R. Recker, and P. D. Saville. "Menopausal Changes in Calcium Balance Performance." *Journal of Laboratory and Clinical Medicine* 92:953–963, 1978.
This paper was the first to show clearly the effect of estrogen on how a middle-aged woman adjusts to the calcium in her diet.

Pennington, J. A. T., and H. N. Church. *Bowes and Church's Food Values of Portions Commonly Used,* 14th edition. Philadelphia: Lippincott, 1985 (257 pages).

> This is THE authoritative source on the nutritional values of foods. Widely used by nutritionists and researchers, it is arranged for easy use.

Young, E. A., editor. *Nutrition, Aging, and Health.* New York: Alan R. Liss, 1986 (280 pages).

> Part of a series on contemporary issues in clinical nutrition, this volume contains chapters on nutrition and the physiology of aging, nutritional assessment of the elderly, and the influence of calcium intake on bone health in older adults.

CALCIUM DEFICIENCY AND OSTEOPOROSIS

FOR THE GENERAL READER

Heaney, R. P. "Osteoporosis." *The World Book Encyclopedia,* 1983.

Osteoporosis. The American Society for Bone and Mineral Research, P.O. Box 739, Kelseyville, CA 95451. 1982.

> The American Society for Bone and Mineral Research is a professional scientific society founded in 1977 and devoted to furthering knowledge in the areas of mineral metabolism and bone disease. This booklet contains guidelines issued by ASBMR.

Osteoporosis: Cause, Treatment, Prevention. Bethesda, Maryland: National Institute of Arthritis and Musculoskeletal and Skin Diseases, National Institutes of Health. NIH publication no. 86-2226. Revised May 1986 (38 pages).

> This pamphlet expands upon the findings of the 1984 National Institutes of Health (NIH) Consensus Panel on Osteoporosis.

SCIENTIFIC BACKGROUND

Avioli, L. V., editor. *The Osteoporotic Syndrome,* 2nd edition. New York: Grune & Stratton, 1987.

> With chapters by eminent scientists in the field, this book summarizes current views about the detection, prevention, and treatment of osteoporosis.

"Osteoporosis." *Journal of the American Medical Association* 52(6):799–802, August 10, 1984.

> This is the text of the report of the 1984 National Institutes of Health (NIH) Consensus Panel on Osteoporosis. The purpose of the conference was to address and reach consensus on specific issues in the prevention and treatment of osteoporosis.

WHAT YOU SHOULD DO

FOR THE GENERAL READER

Dawson-Hughes, B. "How Diet Can Help Prevent Brittle Bones. *Tufts University Diet and Nutrition Letter* 1:3, 1983.

Mayes, K. *Osteoporosis: Brittle Bones and the Calcium Crisis.* Santa Barbara: Pennant Books, 1986 (176 pages).
> Written by a free-lance writer, this book has many practical suggestions both for preventing osteoporosis and for living with osteoporosis when it is present.

From the National Dairy Council (6300 North River Road, Rosemont, IL 60018):

> *Are You at Risk for Bone Disease?* 1984.

> *Like Mother, Like Daughter: A Woman's Guide to Bone Health,* 1985.

> *Sticks and Stones Can Break Your Bones . . . And So Will Too Little Calcium,* 1985.

National Osteoporosis Foundation, 1625 Eye Street NW, Suite 1011, Washington, DC 20006.
> This recently-established national voluntary health agency has four goals:
> - to increase public awareness and knowledge about osteoporosis
> - to provide information to victims of osteoporosis and their families
> - to educate physicians and allied health professionals
> - to support basic biomedical, epidemiological, clinical, behavioral, and social research and research training
>
> The foundation intends to set up a national network of regional chapters.

"Osteoporosis." *Consumer Reports* 49:576, October 1984.
> An excellent, consumer-oriented summary of the osteoporosis story, with value comparisons of several common supplements.

SCIENTIFIC BACKGROUND

Carr, C. J., and R. F. Shangraw. "Nutritional and Pharmaceutical Aspects of Calcium Supplementation." *American Pharmacy,* NS-27, 1987 (pp. 49–57).
> Preparations intended to be used as calcium supplements must break up in the stomach and dissolve in order to be absorbed. Yet some preparations do not do so very readily. This paper contains eye-opening data on how well certain name brand calcium supplements break up and dissolve.

Goodman, C. E. "Osteoporosis: Protective Measures of Nutrition and Exercise." *Geriatrics* 40(4):59–70, April 1985.

This is the source of the drawings that we use to illustrate exercises to avoid and exercises that are recommended for the older woman.

Henderson, B. E., R. K. Ross, A. Paganini-Hill, and T. M. Mack. "Estrogen Use and Cardiovascular Disease." *American Journal of Obstetrics and Gynecology*, June 1986, pp. 1181–1186.

This paper discusses the risks and benefits of estrogen replacement therapy for postmenopausal women. It is the best such analysis yet published.

Index

Accidents, risk of, by older
people, 106–7, 212
Acid rain, 79
"Adaptation, diseases of," 140
Adolescents
calcium RDA for, 74, 75
female, calcium intake of, 94–
97, 112, 183, 208
See also Anorexia nervosa
Adrenal gland, and "diseases of
adaptation," 140
Advertising, 226
for bone scanning, 196
for calcium supplements, 179
Aged persons. *See* Older adults
Aids for daily living, 213–14
Air pollution, 47, 209
Alcohol consumption, 149, 191,
194
for osteoporosis patients, 220
Alka-2 Chewable, 168
Alkali, excessive intake of, 154–55
Allowances
definition of, 71–72
See also Recommended Dietary
Allowances
Almonds
calcium content of, 57, 66
calcium-to-calorie ratio of, 66
cooking with, 159
American Heart Association, 133
Prudent Diet of, 161–63
American Indians, 92
bone record of, 91

American Society for Bone and
Mineral Research, xiv, 227
Amino acids, 233
Anemia, iron and, 109–10
Animals
calcium in, 12, 30–32
mineral deficiencies of, 118
vitamin D absorption by, 44
Anorexia nervosa, 60, 104, 119,
125–27
Antacids, 151, 167
increased loss of urinary calcium
through, 193
for osteoporosis patients, 220
Antlers, formation of, 12, 30–31
Arteries
cholesterol in, 161
supposed calcium deposits in,
155–56
Arthritis, hypertrophic osteo-, 194
Asiatics (Orientals)
bone structures of, 33
milk-sugar intolerance by, 92
Atherosclerosis, 161, 202
Athletes
bone mass of, 34, 35
cessation of menstruation in,
120, 122–23, 207
excessive desire to win by, 207–
9
mineral deficiencies in, 119
Athletic coaches, poor nutritional
information of, 96–97, 209